"I have worked in Indigenous communities for over thirty years, and I wish I'd had Bob Joseph's book at any point over those years. It would have helped me a great deal. It's a very important and valuable book for everyone who works with Indigenous Peoples."

Bruce Falstead, *Manager, Aboriginal Initiatives, FortisBC*

"Fresh off his highly acclaimed and revealing guide to the *Indian Act*, Bob Joseph continues to build bridges between Indigenous and non-Indigenous people with this insightful new book. A guide for developing both corporate and personal relationships, *Indigenous Relations* is an excellent primer for everyone who wants to embark on a new journey of reconciliation and collaboration with Indigenous Peoples, but don't know where—or how—to begin."

Grand Chief Alvin Fiddler, *Nishnawbe Aski Nation*

"The insightful, intelligent, and practical information in this book is of critical importance for building bridges between peoples of different backgrounds, allowing for self-examination on our perspectives and understanding, opening minds and sharpening thinking on inclusiveness, and making reconciliation a reality, which will then bring change."

Lillian Hvatum-Brewster, *Vice President, Indigenous Community Relations & Development, ATCO & Canadian Utilities Limited*

INDIGENOUS RELATIONS

INDIGENOUS RELATIONS

INSIGHTS, TIPS & SUGGESTIONS

TO MAKE

RECONCILIATION A REALITY

BOB JOSEPH WITH CYNTHIA F. JOSEPH

INDIGENOUS
RELATIONS
PRESS

Cataloguing in publication information is available from Library and Archives Canada.

ISBN 978-1-989025-64-2 (paperback)
ISBN 978-1-989025-81-9 (ebook)

Indigenous Relations Press | Page Two Books
www.pagetwo.com

Edited by Amanda Lewis
Copyedited by Tilman Lewis
Proofread by Crissy Calhoun
Cover design by Peter Cocking
Interior design by Taysia Louie
Printed and bound in Canada by Friesens

19 20 21 22 23   5 4 3 2 1

Distributed in Canada by Raincoast Books
www.ictinc.ca

THIS BOOK IS DEDICATED
TO ALL THOSE WHO WANT TO
CHANGE THE WORLD

/\/\/\/\/\/\/\/\/\/\/\/\/\/\/\

WE MUST LEARN TO LIVE TOGETHER...
OR PERISH TOGETHER AS FOOLS.

Dr. Martin Luther King Jr.

Contents

||||||||||||||||||||||||||||||||||||||||||||||

THANKS FOR PICKING UP THIS BOOK.

/\/\/\/\/\/\/\/\/\/\/\/\/\/\/\/\/\/\/\

Doing so shows that you are interested in joining
so many others on the journey to reconciliation.
The insights, tips, and suggestions included
here are all practical and doable. We're sure you
will have some "aha!" moments as you read. You
may even have some "oh no!" moments that make
you squirm. Don't feel bad. We're all on this
learning journey together, and together we will
make this world a better place.

Gilakas'la

BOB JOSEPH
CYNTHIA F. JOSEPH

Moving toward Reconciliation

||||||||||||||||||||||||||||||||||||||||||||||||||||||||||||

AFTER WE PUBLISHED *21 Things You May Not Know About the Indian Act*, a lot of people asked me what they could do to further reconciliation in Canada. *Indigenous Relations* is intended to support that goal of reconciliation by offering practical insights, tips, and suggestions for your business interactions and personal relationships with Indigenous Peoples. While some of this book is intended for the corporate sector, the history, terminology, and advice are of value to all Canadians. It's important for everyone to understand the background to common issues experienced by Indigenous Peoples and communities, from barriers to employment to why protecting the environment long-term is more important than providing employment short-term.

My wife and business partner, Cynthia F. Joseph, and I think of reconciliation as a journey of learning and discovery. By understanding and respecting our cultural differences, we can move toward full reconciliation between

Indigenous and non-Indigenous peoples. By reading this book and working to improve your personal and business relationships, you're taking a step on that journey.

Incorporating reconciliation daily in your life and work is the best way to undo the legacy of the *Indian Act*. The term "reconciliation" carries a great deal of responsibility for a better future, but it also points to the need to recognize the shameful history of Canada's past relationship with Indigenous Peoples as well as the ongoing outcomes of those policies. The path to reconciliation began in 1982 when the rights of Aboriginal Peoples were recognized in Section 35 of Canada's *Constitution Act*. The next milestone on the journey was in 1998 when the federal government made the Statement of Reconciliation, thereby acknowledging government-inflicted damage on Indigenous Peoples. Ten years later, then prime minister Stephen Harper delivered a formal apology to residential school survivors and their families, saying, "The treatment of children in Indian Residential Schools is a sad chapter in our history." However, no substantive improvement in the lives of Indigenous Peoples followed the apology. The government continues to underfund communities and do battle in the courts over Aboriginal Rights, Title, and land claims.

In 2015, the Truth and Reconciliation Commission of Canada (TRC) released its Final Report; the first volume is titled *Honouring the Truth, Reconciling for the Future*.[1] The report, based on the statements of tens of thousands of survivors, shocked many Canadians, who then asked, "Now that I know, what can I do to help right these wrongs?" The TRC's Final Report included ninety-four

Calls to Action, guidelines for moving forward together in a spirit of reconciliation. The Calls to Action cover many sectors such as education, media, and sports. The 92nd Call to Action focuses on how respectful business dealings can contribute to reconciliation.

Business and Reconciliation

92. We call upon the corporate sector in Canada to adopt the *United Nations Declaration on the Rights of Indigenous Peoples* as a reconciliation framework and to apply its principles, norms, and standards to corporate policy and core operational activities involving Indigenous peoples and their lands and resources. This would include, but not be limited to, the following:

   i. Commit to meaningful consultation, building respectful relationships, and obtaining the free, prior, and informed consent of Indigenous peoples before proceeding with economic development projects.

   ii. Ensure that Aboriginal peoples have equitable access to jobs, training, and education opportunities in the corporate sector, and that Aboriginal communities gain long-term sustainable benefits from economic development projects.

   iii. Provide education for management and staff on the history of Aboriginal peoples, including the history and legacy of residential schools, the *United Nations Declaration on the Rights of Indigenous Peoples*, Treaties and Aboriginal rights, Indigenous law, and Aboriginal–Crown relations. This will require skills-based training in intercultural competency, conflict resolution, human rights, and anti-racism.

Reconciliation needs to pair intention with *doing* in order to be effective. So this book offers practical tips for carrying out that 92nd Call to Action. Active reconciliation (sometimes referred to as ReconciliACTION) in Canada consists of honouring treaties and acknowledging and respecting Aboriginal Rights and Title—which could mean returning lands or accepting Indigenous models of self-government.

Many people worry that the common use of "reconciliation" in discussions about decolonizing educational institutions, government agencies, and the legal system, as well as in corporate mandates, could result in it becoming a mere platitude. Without action, reconciliation is yet another empty promise, and over the decades Indigenous Peoples have heard plenty of those—such as to honour the treaties, ensure access to safe drinking water and adequate housing, and establish equity in employment, education, and health care.

This book explores crucial background material, including the *United Nations Declaration on the Rights of Indigenous Peoples* (UNDRIP), terminology, and treaties. It will also give you concrete steps for appropriate relationship building, including making land acknowledgements and following protocols, what to do or say, and what to avoid doing or saying. All of this information is practical and effective. Much of it stems from my decades as an Indigenous relations trainer; much of it stems from being an Indigenous person who has had the benefit of spending time with chiefs, elders, and other prominent Indigenous people; and much comes from being an intergenerational survivor of the residential school system and an Indigenous person who has witnessed and experienced the systemic racism that is the *Indian Act.*

A key first step on your reconciliation journey is to be culturally competent. Many of the TRC's Calls to Action include the common element of training in "cultural competency," which means having the knowledge, skills, and attitude to work across cultures. You might also know this element as intercultural communication or as a commitment to multiculturalism. If you haven't taken Indigenous cultural competency training, such as our training courses, or haven't lived in an Indigenous community, you may lack essential understanding of how integral cultural competency is to reconciliation. This book will help you become more culturally competent by increasing your knowledge of Indigenous Peoples in Canada. Incorporating reconciliation into your work and daily life means acknowledging and letting go of negative perceptions, myths, and stereotypes, so we'll also do some myth busting in this book.

Really, reconciliation means respect—for other people and for yourself in the learning process. To that end, I've included a model of RESPECT (see chapter 8), a step-by-step process that we created and have taught to government at all levels, Fortune 500 companies, resource development corporations, and financial organizations in Canada and around the world. Living respectfully and in alignment with the spirit of reconciliation means taking responsibility—as an individual, parent, student, employee, or employer—to never utter, accept, or ignore a racist comment or stereotype about Indigenous Peoples. Reconciliation means respecting Indigenous individuals, beliefs, cultures, traditions, worldviews, challenges, and goals. It means recognizing and supporting the deep connections Indigenous Peoples have to the natural world and their reclamation of identity, language, culture, and nationhood. Reconciliation is an act of conscious decolonizing of your thinking, actions, and words, and it offers healing for all Canadians and an opportunity to move forward with humility. Let this book be your next step on that journey.

{ 1 }

Indigenous or Aboriginal: Does It Matter?

||||||||||||||||||||||||||||||||||||||||||||||||||||||||||||||||||||||||

DOES IT MATTER if you say "Indigenous" or "Aboriginal"? Well, the short answer is that it does, but terminology can be confusing, and I don't want to bog you down just when you're getting started. So, the section at the end of the book, Terminology: Guidelines for Usage (appendix II), goes into which terms to use in which context.

However, you do need to understand why both "Aboriginal" and "Indigenous" are used in this book, so let's tackle that right up front.

Both terms are derived from Latin and refer to the original inhabitants of the land. And indeed, Indigenous Peoples' creation stories place them here since the dawn of time. Although "Aboriginal" is the term used in the *Constitution Act, 1982*, many Indigenous Peoples prefer the term "Indigenous" as an expression that their communities and cultural groups have lived here since time immemorial. "Aboriginal" is often felt to have a negative connotation, since the prefix "ab-" can mean "not" or "away from" in such words as abnormal or abduct. And "Indigenous" is a self-chosen term rather than a government-imposed one.

While both are umbrella terms, and neither reflects the cultural diversity of Indigenous communities, "Indigenous" is becoming the preferred term. The United Nations uses "Indigenous" to refer to Indigenous populations around the world, although there is not yet a universally accepted definition of "Indigenous Peoples."

There is, however, a working definition. In the 1980s, José Martínez Cobo, the United Nations special rapporteur to the Sub-Commission on Prevention of Discrimination and Protection of Minorities, proposed this working definition of Indigenous communities, peoples, and nations:

> ...those which having a historical continuity with pre-invasion and pre-colonial societies that developed on their territories, consider themselves distinct from other sectors of societies now prevailing in those territories, or parts of them. They form at present non-dominant sectors of society and are determined to preserve, develop, and transmit to future generations their ancestral territories, and their ethnic identity, as the basis of their continued existence as peoples, in accordance with their own cultural patterns, social institutions and legal systems.[1]

But until the terminology in the *Constitution Act* is changed from "Aboriginal" to "Indigenous," we will remain in a state of flux, which I know can be confusing.

In this book, I generally use the term "Aboriginal Peoples" to indicate the collective group of people who hold various rights and obligations under provisions of the Canadian *Constitution Act, 1982*. Additionally, I use "Aboriginal Peoples" in reference to official censuses, in quotations, and in the names of reports.

There are legal reasons for the continued use of the term "Indian"—such as in the *Indian Act* and in government publications that refer to this particular group of Indigenous Peoples. But general usage of the term is considered by many to be derogatory and has been largely replaced by "Indigenous Peoples." When I use "Indigenous Peoples" or "Indigenous communities," in this book, I am referring to First Nations.

Still with me? Good! Let's talk about the importance of recognizing cultural diversity.

{ 2 }

Cultural Diversity among Indigenous Peoples

||||||||||||||||||||||||||||||||||||||||||||||||||||||||||||||||||||||||||||||||||||||||

Anishinaabe, Métis, Coastal Salish, Cree, Cherokee. We have nothing much in common. We're all Aboriginal and we have the drum. That's about it.

Thomas King[1]

WE LIVE IN a multicultural society that recognizes a wide variety of cultures. However, the cultural diversity among the Indigenous population is often overlooked or not realized.

One of the most common mistakes non-Indigenous people make when engaging with Indigenous communities is not recognizing the cultural diversity of Indigenous Peoples. There is a misconception that First Nations are one homogenous group who share the same culture, traditions, language, worldviews, needs, and desires. That could not be further from the truth.

Indigenous communities in Canada are made up of people from many different cultures and languages. A generic or homogenous "Indigenous People of Canada" does not exist. That would be like referring to all people from Europe as "Europeans." When a Scot is asked, "Where did your ancestors come from?" he will answer, "Scotland." If the questioner responds, "Oh, you're European," the Scot may well be offended. It's no different in Indigenous communities. If your response to "I'm from Haida Gwaii" is "Oh, you're Indigenous," you've likely offended the person of Haida ancestry.

Ask a German person what Europeans want, and that German person would probably be able to say what Germans want but not what Europeans want. German interests can be different from other European interests. Similarly, what different Indigenous Peoples want will be as varied as the Indigenous language families and communities they come from; even neighbouring communities may not want the same things at the same time. Therefore, you need to tailor your approach to the particular people and community, even in situations where communities are geographically close or seem to have a similar organizational structure.

In Canada, there are three distinct groups of Aboriginal Peoples: First Nation(s) (sometimes referred to as "Indian"), Métis, and Inuit.[2] More than 1,673,785 of the almost 37 million people in Canada identify as an Indigenous person.[3]

Let's look at the largest group: First Nations. There are over 600 nations and over 2,000 reserves,[4] each with a distinct history that shaped its particular cultural identity.

They also have distinct economies, capacities, and challenges. In British Columbia alone, there is an amazing diversity of First Nations culture and languages. There are over 200 First Nations communities in the province, each with its unique culture, traditions, and history. These 200-plus communities represent 60 per cent of the First Nations languages spoken in Canada.

||||||||||||||||||||||||||||||||||||||||||||||||||||||||||||||||||||||||||||||||||||||||||||||||||||||||||||||||||||||||||||||||||||||||||||||||||||||||

Did you know that, outside of Quebec, English is becoming the common language of Indigenous Peoples in Canada?

||||||||||||||||||||||||||||||||||||||||||||||||||||||||||||||||||||||||||||||||||||||||||||||||||||||||||||||||||||||||||||||||||||||||||||||||||||||||

Linguists refer to language families, which are groups of languages that are clearly distinct yet share enough cognate vocabulary to suggest common ancestry and origin. Canada is home to eleven distinct Indigenous language families, seven of which exist in BC. Each language family is completely distinct; the specific languages within a family may be as similar as French is to Spanish and as different as Czech is to Welsh.

Indigenous Populations

With so many different Indigenous groups, how can we define and measure the Indigenous population in Canada? As with most of the advice in this book, my suggestion is to "ask first." One way to measure the Indigenous population is through a census, like the 2016 Canadian Census. Be advised that there are always at least two troublesome issues when working with statistics: first, how statistics should be interpreted; second, the accuracy of the numbers.

According to the 2016 Canadian Census,[5] 1,673,785 respondents self-identified as an Aboriginal person, which represents 4.9 per cent of the Canadian population. The previous tally was in 2011, at which time the population was 1,400,685 (4.3 per cent of the total population).

> Average age: 32.1 years (40.9 years for
>   non-Indigenous population)
> Children in the 0–4 age range: 145,645
> Adults in the 65 and older range: 122,186

||||||||||||||||||||||||||||||||||||||||||||||||||||||||||||||||||||||||||||||||||||||||||||||||||||||||||||||||||||||||||||||||||||||||||||

Aboriginal Peoples are the fastest-growing segment of the Canadian population. Funding is increasing, but it is not keeping up with the pace of demand.

||||||||||||||||||||||||||||||||||||||||||||||||||||||||||||||||||||||||||||||||||||||||||||||||||||||||||||||||||||||||||||||||||||||||||||

Impact of Urban Migration

In 1991, the federal government created the Royal Commission on Aboriginal Peoples (RCAP) to examine the relationships between the government and Indigenous Peoples and between Indigenous and non-Indigenous people. RCAP was also tasked with advising the government on its findings. In 1996, after four years of consultation, testimony, and research studies, including 178 days of public hearings and ninety-six community visits, the five-volume Report of the Royal Commission on Aboriginal Peoples was released.

The RCAP report noted that migration of Canada's Indigenous population to urban areas was steadily increasing and that serious on-reserve/off-reserve inequities already existed regarding provision of services and benefits. In 2019, that migration continues, as does its impact. RCAP cited three key issues that are still applicable twenty-three years later:

> First, urban Aboriginal people do not receive the same level of services and benefits that First Nations people living on-reserve or Inuit living in their communities obtain from the federal government. Many status people who have moved to the city believe they are disadvantaged because they are not eligible to receive all the services to which they had access on-reserve. Métis people have little access to federal programs because the federal government has been unwilling to acknowledge its Constitutional responsibility for them.
>
> Second, urban Aboriginal people often have difficulty gaining access to provincial programs available to other residents. Some provincial authorities operate on the principle that the federal government should take responsibility for all status Indians, regardless of where they live. Many individual service providers simply do not know what programs—federal, provincial, territorial or municipal—are available to Aboriginal people.
>
> Third, although urban Aboriginal people are eligible for federal and provincial services and programs that

are available to all citizens, they would like access to culturally appropriate programs that would meet their needs more effectively.[6]

This urban migration means that some of your outreach engagement will occur on reserves but will also be required to extend to include community members who have relocated to urban settings.

||||||||||||||||||||||||||||||||||||||||||||||||||||||||||||||||||||||||||||||||||||||||||||||||||||||||||||||||||||||

There is no "one size fits all" approach when it comes to outreach or helping to solve challenges. Customize accordingly.

||||||||||||||||||||||||||||||||||||||||||||||||||||||||||||||||||||||||||||||||||||||||||||||||||||||||||||||||||||||

Recognizing the unique history, culture, and traditions of each community is a fundamental first step that Canadians can take to respect Indigenous Peoples. Take the time to get to know local Indigenous communities and those you are working with.

Indigenous Relations Tips

- I think just about every Indigenous community now has a website, so that's a good place to start your learning. Some websites include population figures, business listings, departments, and the names of the chief and council. If you look closely at the list of committees, you will learn the primary issues of that community.

- Attend a public cultural event, also often listed on the website. Showing your appreciation of an Indigenous community's culture is respectful. Encourage your whole team to attend, but be aware that not all cultural events are open to the public. When in doubt, ask.

- Research the protocol associated with the event. For example, if you are going to attend a powwow, understand the protocol around touching the regalia (and it's called regalia, not a costume) or taking photos. It's strictly forbidden to drink alcohol at a powwow.

- Learn about the community's artists and consider purchasing some art for your office.

- Volunteer in the community. If, for example, the community is having a beach cleaning event, contact the community's office to see if you are welcome to help. Encourage your whole team to join you and offer to bring your own supplies, provide transport, or contribute to snacks and beverages.

{ 3 }

Indigenous Identity and Governance Structure

||||||||||||||||||||||||||||||||||||||||||||||||||||||||||||||||||||||||||||||||||||||||||||||||||||

AT THE TIME of European contact, the continents now called North and South America were inhabited by many diverse Indigenous Peoples, representing a wide range of values, beliefs, and religious views. Clearly defined geographic boundaries and the abundance of fish, wildlife, and natural resources allowed many Indigenous communities to develop distinct, thriving cultures and languages. Each community had its own social structure, legal system, and political system.

Indigenous Governance Structures in Canada: Hereditary or Traditional, or Elected

Prior to European contact, Indigenous societies in Canada used different governance structures. Scholars have transcribed oral histories of matrilineal, patrilineal, and egalitarian nation governments. In matrilineal communities, women held the balance of power; in patrilineal communities, men did.

In the 1880s, Section 74 was inserted into the *Indian Act*, imposing a regime for the election of chiefs and band councils under a system of rules patterned after municipal law. Over the years, many First Nations strenuously opposed this imposition of a foreign governance structure. Where such structures have been imposed, they have often contributed to breakdowns of traditional communal culture and governance and to destructive class divisions within communities.

One issue with the elected chief system is that chiefs are elected by the community, but their role is to administer the *Indian Act*. They work for the federal government, not for the people who elected them. Another is the imposed frequency of elections. Initially, elections were mandated annually, then the election cycle was extended to every two years. The continual manoeuvring for power can be very disruptive to community harmony, especially in communities with smaller memberships. It can pit family members against one another as they vie for leadership.

Over the years, many nations were able to maintain their customary and hereditary governance cultures, often running alongside or "behind" the elected band council. More recently, many nations have taken advantage of *Indian Act* amendments in 1985, allowing a return to traditional and hereditary governance structures and systems.[1]

‖‖

There are two classifications of chief:

Hereditary or traditional chief: A leader who has power passed down from one generation to the next along bloodlines or other cultural protocols that are similar to European royalty.

Elected chief: A person elected by band members to govern for a specified term. Under the specifications of the *Indian Act*, First Nations must have an election every two or sometimes three years.

Please note that "chief" is a European term. Traditional leaders can go by many titles, including headmen/women, clan leaders, and heads of villages or groups of people. Titles and roles are passed along a community-driven protocol.

Each nation had its own pre-contact system of governance that had been developing for thousands of years or, in my personal context and many others like it, since time immemorial. These governance structures weren't granted by other governments. That means that we, as Indigenous Peoples, have an inherent right to self-government. This is a right given to us by the Creator and not granted by any other government. At Confederation, Canada began its assimilation policy, consolidated the *Indian Act*, and moved to replace hereditary or traditional forms of governance with elected chiefs and councils. This action of replacing traditional leadership represents a direct imposition on self-governing communities that requires them to elect a chief and council and forgo their traditional systems of governance. (We'll go into self-government more in chapter 6.)

Since that time, some people—including me—have sought to return to our traditional and, in my case, inherited forms of governance. In the past, this action would clearly be against the goal of the *Indian Act* (assimilation) and by extension, the wishes of the Canadian federal government. But as Canada has abandoned forced cultural assimilation, we will continue to move to self-government in all its different forms. In July 2017, then justice minister Jody Wilson-Raybould told the Assembly of First Nations that First Nations should prepare for a future in which *Indian Act* bands are phased out and the door is opened to more traditional governance.[2]

Some communities may return to their traditional inherent governments and others may wish to proceed with an elected style of self-government. We may even see some blend their inherited models of government with the democratic process, as England did with its monarchy and parliament.

Of course, while all of this is unfolding, you still need to have conversations or do consultations with peoples who have not moved fully to self-government. The dichotomy between elected councils and hereditary chiefs is important for understanding which leaders to talk to and how to address them. The question becomes: who do you talk to, the elected chief and councils or hereditary or traditional leadership? In some communities, it will be the elected chief and council, as the community sees them as having legal and legitimate authority. In other communities, when it comes to lands and resource use, you may be talking to hereditary chiefs as represented in organizations such as the office of the Gitxsan Hereditary Chiefs, for example. The Gitxsan Hereditary Chiefs have been clear all along that they make decisions about lands and resources, and band chiefs and councils look after federally mandated programs like health care, housing, and education as funded by the Department of Crown-Indigenous Relations and Northern Affairs Canada (CIRNAC).

One challenge with a combined hereditary and elected leadership structure is that it can be unclear who makes decisions on behalf of the people. In 2019, CIRNAC Minister Carolyn Bennett referenced the *Indian Act* as the source for confusion over who had authority to speak for the community: "I think that we're in this transition, hopefully, transformation, to be able to get more and more communities out from under the *Indian Act,* so that there isn't this question of who speaks for the community, as they choose a governance of their own making."[3] Again, an indication of the importance of moving toward a return to self-government.

What happens if the hereditary and elected leaders don't get along and both claim to be the decision makers? In such cases where it is unclear who has the legitimate and legal authority to make decisions, my advice to corporate and government clients is to talk to the whole community and get community support.

Before commencing negotiations and before relying on band council decisions, companies and government officials should prepare by learning the particular community's leadership and decision-making protocols and then protect themselves by confirming that the prescribed decision-making procedures were followed.

Indigenous Relations Tips

- *Research, research, research* so that you have a strong picture of the governance within the community.

- If there are elected and hereditary chiefs, engage with both, and do so with equal effort. Recognize both if you host a meeting.

- Learn the election cycle. How frequent are elections? (Typically, every two or three years.) If you are beginning your engagement with a community that is nearing the end of its election cycle, be careful who you align yourself with. If you are seen as being on the side of the outgoing chief, then you could have some hard work ahead of you to establish a relationship with the incoming chief.

{ 4 }

Circle of Understanding: Recognizing Indigenous Worldviews

IIIIIIIIIIIIIIIIIIIIIIIIIIIIIIIIIIIIIIIIIIIIIIIIIIII

Any individual within a culture is going to have his or her own personal interpretation of the collective cultural code; however, the individual's worldview has its roots in the culture—that is, in the society's shared philosophy, values, and customs. If we are to understand why Aboriginal and Eurocentric worldviews clash, we need to understand how the philosophy, values, and customs of Aboriginal cultures differ from those of Eurocentric cultures.

Dr. Leroy Little Bear, member of the Blackfoot
Confederacy, professor emeritus and special advisor to the
President's Office at the University of Lethbridge[1]

FIRST OF ALL, what is a worldview? A worldview is a way of knowing, seeing, explaining, and living in the world. It encompasses considerations such as distinct values and different ideas about what is important in life.

Primer on Indigenous Worldviews

Here are five common threads found in Indigenous worldviews:

- Holistic perspective
- Unified vision
- All life is sacred
- All forms of life are interconnected
- Humans are not above or below others

All living things, including plants and animals, and their spirits are connected or related—law, kinship, and spirituality reinforce this connectedness. Our actions and decisions affect all else in the circle of life. All individuals are responsible for themselves in relation to all others.

The well-being of the earth is central to traditional teachings and practices and is essential for survival.

Time is fluid, non-linear, and measured in relation to cyclical events—the seasons.

Indigenous cultures are guided by tradition and collected wisdom, yet are dynamic, adaptive, and not relegated to the past.

Adaptation has been and continues to be necessary for survival.

Our world is multicultural, with a corresponding plethora of worldviews. Understanding the many traditions, beliefs, and practices of other cultures, and how those attributes differ from your own, contributes to mutual respect, tolerance, and cultural harmony. Understanding the core differences between Indigenous worldviews and Western worldviews is a critical component of achieving respectful relationships with Indigenous Peoples.

The root difference between Indigenous and Western worldviews is that they generally adhere to opposite approaches to knowledge, connectedness, and science. Indigenous cultures focus on a holistic understanding of the whole that emerged from the millennia of their existence and experiences. Traditional Western worldviews tend to be more concerned with science and concentrate on compartmentalized knowledge and then move on to understanding the bigger, related picture. Indigenous Peoples' worldviews are based on the circle, whereas Western worldviews are pyramidal in form, with humans at the top. In one, all living things are equal; in the other, there is a hierarchy.

> Envision, if you will, a circle. The Creator occupies the centre of the circle and society... revolves around the Creator.
>
> This system is not based on hierarchy. Rather, it is based on harmony. Harmony between the elements, between and within ourselves and within our relationship with the Creator. In this circle there are only equals.
>
> Now, envision a triangle. This triangle represents the fundamental elements of the Euro-Canadian society.

Authority emanates from the top and filters down to the bottom. Those at the bottom are accountable to those at the top, that is control. Control in this society is not self-imposed, but rather exercised by those at the top upon those beneath them.

In this system the place of the First Nations peoples is at the bottom. This is alien to the fundamental elements of our society, where we are accountable only to the Creator, our own consciences and to the maintenance of harmony."

CHIEF TONY MERCREDI, Athabasca Chipewyan
First Nation Community, Fort Chipewyan, Alberta[2]

Working across cultures means recognizing and respecting each other's different life experiences, goals, ideals, values, challenges, beliefs, family relationships, and so on. We are not all the same, and one is not better than the other.

Are Indigenous People Pro-Development or Pro-Conservation?

In my training sessions, I'm often asked if Indigenous people are pro-development or pro-conservation. My answer is "It depends." Two considerations come into play in evaluating a community's views on development or conservation: belief structures and socio-economic conditions.

To begin this discussion, we must consider the history of Indigenous communities in North America. Many scholars, until recently, believed that the Indigenous Peoples who populated North America did so by way of a land bridge that stretched across the Bering Sea. The land bridge theory considers a single wave of migration from

Asia at the end of the last ice age as being responsible for the population of North and South America. Mention this theory to Indigenous communities and ask them if they crossed a land bridge, and their response would likely be "No." Indigenous communities generally believe that they came to these lands through creation, not via a land bridge. This belief is supported by their respective first ancestor or creation stories.

Creation is an important belief in trying to determine whether an Indigenous community is pro-development or pro-conservation. From a worldview that takes creation into consideration, Indigenous communities were given lands by the Creator. These lands were to be used and protected for the Indigenous communities' benefit and are required for their long-term cultural survival for the next ten thousand years and beyond. It is this ability for cultural and individual survival that Indigenous communities use as their measure of sustainability in an ideal world, and it suggests a pro-conservation belief.

Unfortunately, this is not an ideal world. A look at current socio-economic conditions in Indigenous communities is a second consideration. What do the key indicators show in a community? Is there high or low unemployment? Are there high rates of suicide and violence because of a lack of economic opportunities? What health issues are affecting the community? If an Indigenous community is wrestling with poor socio-economic conditions, and many (but not all) are, they may be more inclined to address short-term socio-economic issues through natural resource development.

Put another way, the need to survive culturally in the short-term can push Indigenous communities to be more pro-development. However, it is not development at any cost. Indigenous communities will still weigh their development decisions against long-term cultural survival. Often the Seventh Generation Principle will be an influencing factor. This principle, based on an ancient Iroquois philosophy that the decisions we make today should result in a sustainable world seven generations into the future, can also be applied to relationships—every decision should result in sustainable relationships seven generations into the future. (See the Strategize component of the RESPECT model in chapter 8 for more information on the Seventh Generation Principle.)

Indigenous Relations Tips

- Don't assume that because Indigenous worldviews share similarities, they are all the same.

- Respecting Indigenous worldviews is as important in your workplace culture as it is in on-site project consultation.

- In consultation meetings, don't talk about Western science as though it is the de facto authority.

- Everything in Indigenous worldviews is connected, so be careful with your claims that your project in one area won't have an impact elsewhere. Heed the lesson of a major pipeline project that was denied approval because the community raised the issue of whales, and government representatives had not included that discussion in the scope of project review.

Working with Communities: Employment Barriers and Other Issues

IIIIIIIIIIIIIIIIIIIIIIIIIIIIIIIIIIIIIIIIIIIIIIIIIIIIIIIIIIIIIIIIIIIII

I F WE ARE going to achieve the goal of reconciliation, then we must all understand where people are coming from and be prepared to acknowledge uncomfortable truths about Canadian history. Indigenous Peoples bring a lot of history with them to the reconciliation conversation.

Here's what history—i.e., post-contact—looks like from an Indigenous perspective:

invisible: The Doctrine of Discovery provided a framework for Christian explorers, in the name of their sovereign, to lay claim to territories uninhabited by Christians. If the lands were vacant, then they could be defined as "discovered" and sovereignty could be claimed. When Christopher Columbus arrived in North America in 1492, the Indigenous Peoples, as non-Christians, were invisible.

31

savages: The Fathers of Confederation, including our first prime minister John A. Macdonald, referred to Indigenous Peoples as "savages" in official documents.

erased: Duncan Campbell Scott, deputy superintendent general of Indian Affairs, in 1920 stated, "Our objective is to continue until there is not a single Indian in Canada that has not been absorbed into the body politic."[1]

not people: At the midpoint of the previous century, when the *Indian Act* was revised in 1951, Aboriginal Peoples were finally—legally—acknowledged as people. Earlier versions of the *Indian Act* read, "The term 'person' means an individual other than an Indian, unless the context clearly requires another construction."[2]

The Lasting Impact of the Doctrine of Discovery

The Truth and Reconciliation Commission's 94 Calls to Action, released in 2015, included suggestions for overriding the idea of the Doctrine of Discovery in government and faith organizations:

45. We call upon the Government of Canada, on behalf of all Canadians, to jointly develop with Aboriginal peoples a Royal Proclamation of

Reconciliation to be issued by the Crown. The proclamation would build on the Royal Proclamation of 1763 and the Treaty of Niagara of 1764, and reaffirm the nation-to-nation relationship between Aboriginal peoples and the Crown. The proclamation would include, but not be limited to, the following commitments:

i. Repudiate concepts used to justify European sovereignty over Indigenous lands and peoples such as the Doctrine of Discovery and *terra nullius*…

46. We call upon the parties to the Indian Residential Schools Settlement Agreement to develop and sign a Covenant of Reconciliation that would identify principles for working collaboratively to advance reconciliation in Canadian society, and that would include, but not be limited to:…

ii. Repudiation of concepts used to justify European sovereignty over Indigenous lands and peoples, such as the Doctrine of Discovery and *terra nullius,* and the reformation of laws, governance structures, and policies within their respective institutions that continue to rely on such concepts…

47. We call upon federal, provincial, territorial, and municipal governments to repudiate concepts used to justify European sovereignty over Indigenous peoples and lands, such as the Doctrine of Discovery and *terra nullius,* and to reform those laws, government policies, and litigation strategies that continue to rely on such concepts...

49. We call upon all religious denominations and faith groups who have not already done so to repudiate concepts used to justify European sovereignty over Indigenous lands and peoples, such as the Doctrine of Discovery and *terra nullius.*

Generally, until relatively recently, Indigenous perspectives on history were not taught in mainstream schools, and residential schools were run in isolation. For most Canadians, the only time they saw Indigenous Peoples was in stereotypical roles in movies or in the news. And if they were in the news, it was because they were "drumming, dancing, drunk, or dead,"[3] as an elder put it to broadcaster Duncan McCue. So the view that mainstream Canadians had of Indigenous Peoples was in relation to "their" problems, which were not seen to result from the impacts of government policies of cultural genocide and assimilation but rather from a weakness of character or an inferior society or culture.

The ongoing impacts of colonialism are never far from the surface. When working with Indigenous Peoples and communities, it is critical that you initiate and develop your relationship with an awareness of those impacts. If, for example, your mandate is to develop for your organization a recruitment and retention strategy or an Impact and Benefit Agreement (IBA) that includes employment (and most will), then you have to understand the history behind the lower-than-average education attainment levels, why having a pair of steel-toed boots might be out of the question, why not having a driver's licence is an impediment to arriving at work on time, and why seasonal activities and community commitments may take precedence over punching the clock.

It would help you to learn about the history, worldview, culture, values, and traditions of each community that you work with. It is not their responsibility to teach you. Many communities do not have the time or resources to bring every contractor or liaison officer up to speed on who they are. And why should they? You are asking to work with them. Hence the requirement of cultural competency training.

Priority Issues

Seven of the key issues that are of greatest concern for Indigenous Peoples in Canada are complex and inexorably intertwined—so much so that government, researchers, policy makers, and Indigenous leaders seem frozen by their enormity. It is hard to isolate just one issue as being the worst. The *Indian Act* greatly contributes to these seven issues and more. (If you'd like to learn more about the intent and extent of the Act, read my 2018 book *21 Things You May Not Know About the Indian Act*.)

These issues of community distress dominate leadership thinking in Canada. Indigenous leaders and negotiators will tend to place premium value on measures that increase levels of health, education, housing, and income in their communities, as well as on measures that decrease levels of unemployment, incarceration, substance abuse, and suicide.

1. POORER HEALTH

The World Health Organization's investigation into health determinants now recognizes European colonization as a common and fundamental underlying determinant of Indigenous health. While great strides have been made by many Indigenous communities to improve education around health issues, Indigenous Peoples continue to experience higher rates of diabetes, heart disease, tuberculosis, HIV/AIDS, and many other diseases.[4] There are definite links between income, social factors, and health. There is a higher rate of respiratory problems and other infectious diseases among Indigenous children than among non-Indigenous children; inadequate housing and crowded living conditions are contributing factors.

2. LOWER LEVELS OF EDUCATION

According to the 2016 Canadian Census, 33.65 per cent of those who identified as an Aboriginal person have no secondary (high) school or equivalency certificate, compared to 18.3 per cent of the rest of the Canadian population.[5]

3. INADEQUATE HOUSING AND CROWDED LIVING CONDITIONS

Three words: Attawapiskat First Nation. In 2011, the conditions in this community drew national and international media attention—as well as the attention of the United Nations—to a housing situation that far too many Indigenous communities struggle with. Of those First Nations people living on-reserve, 44.2 per cent lived in a dwelling that was in need of major repairs, compared to 6 per cent of the non-Indigenous population living in such a dwelling.[6]

4. LOWER INCOME LEVELS

The average total income of Indigenous Peoples was 75 per cent that of non-Indigenous people in 2015—that's a 25 per cent income gap. It is a slight improvement from the 27 per cent gap ten years before in 2005.[7]

5. HIGHER LEVELS OF INCARCERATION

In 2015–2016, Indigenous adults were overrepresented in admissions to provincial and territorial correctional services. They accounted for 26 per cent of admissions, while representing only about 3 per cent of the Canadian adult population. In federal correctional services, Indigenous adults accounted for 28 per cent of admissions to custody.

Indigenous females were more overrepresented than males. Indigenous females accounted for 38 per cent of female admissions to provincial and territorial sentenced custody; the comparable figure for Indigenous males was 26 per cent. In federal correctional services, Indigenous females accounted for 31 per cent of female admissions to sentenced custody, while the figure for Indigenous males was 23 per cent.[8]

6. HIGHER RATES OF SUICIDE

Most tragic of all is the higher rate of suicide among First Nations, Métis, and Inuit youth. A 2016 Statistics Canada report found that more than one in five off-reserve First Nations, Métis, and Inuit adults reported having suicidal thoughts at some point in their lives. Suicide rates are five to seven times higher for First Nations youth than for non-Aboriginal youth, and for Inuit youth, the rate is among the highest in the world—*eleven times the national average*. A Health Canada report on 2000 statistics stated, "Suicide and self-inflicted injuries are the leading causes of death for First Nations youth and adults up to 44 years of age."[9]

7. HIGHER RATES OF UNEMPLOYMENT

Indigenous Peoples have historically faced higher unemployment rates than non-Indigenous people. The employment rates of Indigenous Peoples in Canada did not increase between 2006 and 2016.[10]

Barriers to Employment

Barriers—some tangible, some intangible—maintain the status quo of exorbitant rates of unemployment among Indigenous Peoples in Canada. Historically, through the

Indian Act and its outcomes, Indigenous Peoples have been socially, geographically, politically, educationally, and economically excluded.

The 1936 *Annual Report of the Department of Indian Affairs* read:

> During the past fiscal year, many of the Indians of Canada found it necessary to seek assistance from the department in food and clothing due to unemployment and sickness. The Indian was the first to be thrown out of work when the depression started and evidently will be the last to be again absorbed when conditions improve. There seems to be a tendency on the part of employers of labour to **refuse employment to Indians considering that they are a public charge and it is not necessary to give them employment where there are white applicants for the job.**[11] [emphasis added]

Fast-forward to the 2008 economic downturn, and the "first out" trend was still very much apparent.[12] So, what are the most common barriers?

1. **Literacy and education:** Among young First Nations adults living off-reserve, the high school completion rate is 75 per cent. But among those living on-reserve, only 48 per cent—less than half—have completed high school. If the on-reserve high school completion rate rises six points every five years, then in thirty-five years it will match the rate for non-Indigenous young adults.[13]

2. **Cultural differences:** Employers and co-workers may not understand or respect the unique cultural differences of Indigenous Peoples, which can create a worksite

atmosphere of disrespect, resentment, or distrust. (Review the material on respecting cultural diversity and worldviews in chapters 2 and 4.)

3. **Racism, discrimination, and stereotypes:** Assumptions about Indigenous Peoples are fundamental barriers to Indigenous workers getting a job and remaining in the job, and they are directly related to attitudes passed down since European settlers arrived in North America. Some non-Indigenous people believe a number of myths and misconceptions about Indigenous Peoples and perceived special treatment. We'll look at some of these myths in chapter 7.

4. **Self-esteem:** Poverty, broken families, racism, stereotypes, discrimination, and few positive role models all contribute to low self-esteem. It's hard to present well in a job interview when you are struggling with low self-esteem.

5. **Poverty and poor housing:** Of the 1,673,785 people who reported an Aboriginal identity on the 2016 Canadian Census, 324,900 lived in a dwelling that was in need of major repairs. This group accounted for one-fifth (19.4 per cent) of the total Aboriginal population in Canada. In comparison, 6 per cent of the non-Aboriginal population reported living in a dwelling in need of major repairs.[14] Unhealthy living conditions affect a person's mental and physical well-being.

6. **Lack of a driver's licence:** Not having a driver's licence can be a real stumbling block in remote communities; it can be a challenge just to get to the nearest office to write the initial test. Taking driver's training is

similarly a challenge. There may be no easily accessed training providers or, for that matter, vehicles in which to learn.

7. **Transportation:** Few remote communities are serviced by public transit; vehicle insurance is expensive and out of reach for many in pre-employment situations. Again, potential employees frequently do not own or have access to a vehicle.

8. **Child care:** Safe, affordable child care is a challenge for most people in Canada. It's even more of a challenge for parents in Indigenous communities.

Massive, comprehensive studies have been done on these issues for years, yet sadly the barriers identified decades ago are pretty much the same in 2019. There is not a lot of traction on the ground in terms of change and improvement.

It is in the best interests of all Canadians for the employment rates of Indigenous Peoples to significantly improve, because "all governments in Canada are losing an estimated $8.4 billion annually as a result of the poverty rate gap between Indigenous people and the non-Indigenous population."[15] It continues to be a struggle to reach the point where Indigenous Peoples are considered valued employees and part of an inclusive and culturally diverse workplace.

The Bottom Line

Indigenous Peoples represent a considerable market as consumers of goods and services. And just like other consumers of goods and services, they are more likely to take their business to service providers and stores in which they are comfortable, feel welcome, and see themselves reflected in the faces of the staff and management.

If you were an Indigenous business owner, would you take your business to a financial institution that has Indigenous employees or to one that is culturally exclusive? If you were an Indigenous economic development officer looking for an engineering firm, would you be more inclined to take your business to a company that has employees that look like you or to one that has no Indigenous engineers? If you were a talented, ambitious Indigenous law graduate, would you join a company whose partners all share a similar hue and background?

The gains of including Indigenous Peoples in your workforce include improved relations with Indigenous communities, stimulating the local economy, and increasing the base of qualified workers. If your operation is remote, hiring locally is the right and cost-efficient thing to do.

In the resource sector, having Indigenous individuals on your team and in the boardroom can be advantageous in terms of your relations with the Indigenous communities you are working with. Let's look at the example of a mining company entering into the consultation phase of a major project. Consultation is a complex process that must take into account the tangible impact on economic, employment, and education opportunities. But consultation also requires considering the social and spiritual impacts on affected communities. It will be invaluable to have team members who understand Indigenous perspectives and influences on decision-making. If your consultation strategy includes Indigenous individuals at every level, the community is likely to feel more comfortable in their dealings with your company.

One of the challenges to retaining Indigenous employees is that many worksites are not inclusive environments. Creating a working environment that embraces inclusive principles is a foundation for retaining Indigenous workers.

Indigenous Relations Tips

- Involve your existing workforce in learning about what makes a workplace inclusive. Hold brainstorming sessions on how your company can create an inclusive work environment.

- Don't expect an Indigenous employee to be an expert on all Indigenous Peoples, cultures, histories, and so on. They will likely be unwilling to speak of cultures other than their own.

- Research the culture of the Indigenous community you want to draw workers from. Culture is often equated to an iceberg—the part we see above the water is a small fraction of what lies beneath. To understand the culture of the local community, you need to look below the surface. Learn about the history of the community and its leadership structure and traditions, and then educate your existing workforce on the local Indigenous community culture. For inclusiveness to be accepted, it needs to be ingrained throughout your organization from the boardroom down.

- Provide Indigenous awareness or Indigenous relations training for the existing workforce. There is much about Indigenous Peoples that non-Indigenous people tend not to understand. Awareness training can go a long way to ameliorating actions that can adversely affect a new employee, right from the opening handshake. You'll see more on what not to say or do in chapter 8.

- Provide educational programs that allow Indigenous employees the opportunity to upgrade basic skills if needed. Lower levels of numeracy and literacy and sub-standard education are barriers to workplace success. Opening the window to skills upgrading opportunities and career advancement is a good indicator that a worker is considered a valued member of the company.

{ **6** }

Nation to Nation: Understanding Treaties, Then and Now

IIIIIIIIIIIIIIIIIIIIIIIIIIIIIIIIIIIIIIIIIIIIIIIIIIIIIIIIIIIIIIIIIII

IN YOUR RELATIONSHIPS with Indigenous communities, you may find yourself conversing in the language of treaties—whether you are creating policy or offering a land acknowledgement. But what are treaties, and what role do they play for Indigenous communities today?

Treaties are negotiated government-to-government contracts or agreements, used to define rights and powers and to formalize relations between governments. Since contact, Indigenous Peoples have been negotiating treaties on a nation-to-nation basis. The Royal Proclamation of 1763 acknowledged "several Nations or Tribes of Indians with whom We are connected," and by doing so recognized Indigenous Peoples as nations.

The idea of "nations" comes from King George III and his colonial government and confirms the international convention of the day that colonizing countries that reached inhabited lands were to conduct business with the inhabitants on a nation-to-nation basis and treat those inhabitants as owners of the lands. "Nation to nation" means a government can exercise its jurisdictions without interference from other governments.

Historic and numbered treaties cover much of the central corridor of Canada. Many of the early treaties are referred to as Peace and Friendship Treaties. When looking at historic treaties, keep in mind the era and the intent of the parties involved. From the perspective of the Indigenous leaders who "marked" the treaties (they did not sign them—as an oral society that depended on people honouring their verbal commitment, signing a document was an alien concept), they knew that their world and the world for future generations of their people was changing.

Historic treaties form the basis of the relationship between the Crown and 364 First Nations.

- Treaties of Peace and Neutrality (1701–1760)
- Peace and Friendship Treaties (1725–1779)
- Upper Canada Land Surrenders and the Williams Treaties (1764–1862/1923)
- Robinson Treaties and Douglas Treaties (1850–1854)
- The Numbered Treaties (1871–1921)

The modern treaty era began in 1973 after a Supreme Court of Canada decision (*Calder et al. v. Attorney-General of British Columbia*) recognized Aboriginal Rights for the first time. This decision led to the development of the Comprehensive Land Claims Policy and the modern treaties, including the James Bay and Northern Québec Agreement (signed in 1975), the Inuvialuit Final Agreement (signed in 1984), and the Nisga'a Final Agreement (1999).

Indigenous leaders negotiated in good faith for the survival of their people as they transitioned from their formerly expansive self-determining, self-governing, and self-reliant world to subsistence and dependence, living on small reserves. The treaty articles they negotiated included education, economic assistance, health care, livestock, agriculture tools, and agricultural training.

The other signatory, the Crown, had a different intent. Under John A. Macdonald, Canada's first prime minister, the Crown planned to use the treaties to remove Indigenous Peoples from their lands, gain access to natural resources, open up the country for settlers, and construct a railway from Upper Canada (predecessor of modern Ontario) to the Pacific Ocean.

As Bob Rae put it in 2014 remarks to the University of Regina:

> From the perspective of the government of Canada and of provinces, what the treaties said was this: First Nations give up all claim to the land, surrender absolutely any claim to the land, in exchange for which they would get, depending on the treaty, either 4 dollars or 5 dollars a year, the right to continue to live on a reserve, the right to continue to hunt on traditional territory and some sense that they were being protected by the crown.[1]

In 1991, Canada created the Indian Claims Commission as an independent tribunal to hear Indigenous communities' specific land claims, which arose from federal treaties and had been rejected by the federal government. The commission was based on a model proposed by Indigenous organizations.

The Government of Canada has negotiated several modern treaties, or comprehensive land claim settlements as they are sometimes called, including the James Bay and Northern Québec Agreement and the Inuvialuit Final Agreement. These modern treaties have been negotiated with the purpose of fulfilling Canada's constitutional obligations to Aboriginal Peoples. Section 35 (3) of the *Constitution Act, 1982*, states "'treaty rights' includes the rights that now exist by way of land claims agreements or may be so acquired."

Three important components of treaties will be sorted out as communities move to final agreements: self-determination, self-reliance, and self-government.

Self-Determination

Self-determination is the right to decide who your people are. A major objective of Indigenous Peoples, country-wide, is to gain control over who belongs to their nation. Currently, bands are required to maintain a registry, with many of the rules governing membership mandated by the *Indian Act*. As we move forward, the desire is for communities, rather than a bureaucrat in Ottawa, to decide who their members are.

Self-Reliance

Another key objective for Indigenous Peoples is self-reliance. They want the ability to participate in the political and, more importantly, the economic mainstream, without having to rely on federal funding through CIRNAC and Indigenous Services to meet community needs, for which they are chronically underfunded. As noted earlier, the Indigenous population is growing but the funding is not keeping pace. In cases such as the Nisga'a Final Agreement (1999), the nation agreed that it would pay taxes in exchange for taxpayer equity funding for programs available to other taxpayers. For example, prior to the self-government agreement, the nation received less funding for K–12 education than did the taxpayers in nearby communities. With the Final Agreement, it now receives taxpayer equity funding for K–12 education.

The Report of the Royal Commission on Aboriginal Peoples reads: "At the heart of our recommendations is recognition that Aboriginal peoples are peoples, that they form collectivities of unique character, and that they have a right of governmental autonomy."[2]

Other aspects of self-reliance include communities seeking business opportunities and getting into the realm of collecting taxes, royalties, and revenue sharing on land developments—all of which are viewed as key pieces of the self-reliance objective.

Self-Government

Without self-government, the *Indian Act* governs the day-to-day operations of a nation, which can include looking after housing, health care, and education. As noted earlier, while band councils and chiefs are elected by their people, they are accountable to CIRNAC. The preference of many nations is to change to a system in which the governing leaders are elected and accountable to their people, instead of to the Crown. Such models do exist, and communities with self-government agreements have done well in the nation-building process.

Self-government agreements can be stand-alone agreements, or self-government provisions can be included in treaties. For example, Westbank First Nation ratified a self-government agreement in 2005. It gave power to Westbank for the purposes of employment, education, economy, housing, language, and culture. The nation has not yet signed a treaty, so the agreement does not apply to treaty lands; it applies mostly to reserve lands. The Nisga'a treaty included lands, resources, and provisions for governance via the Nisga'a Lisims Government of those lands and resources.

INHERENT RIGHT TO SELF-GOVERNMENT

This authority is not something bestowed by other governments. It is inherent in their identity as peoples. But to be fully effective, their authority must be recognized by other governments.

Report of the Royal Commission on Aboriginal Peoples[3]

For many years, the Government of Canada refused even to entertain the concept of Aboriginal self-government. That policy mountain moved in 1973, shortly after the release of the Supreme Court of Canada's landmark decision in the *Calder* case.[4] Even then, the government sought to narrow the interpretation and restrict the scope of Aboriginal self-government to a legislatively based approach: to ensure that any form of self-government that might result from negotiations would come into existence as a legislative grant by the Parliament of Canada and would therefore operate "at the pleasure of Parliament"— that is, subject to parliamentary amendment.

The final volume of the five-volume Report of the Royal Commission on Aboriginal Peoples opened with a sketch of the social, health, economic, and governance problems that confront many Indigenous communities—in their internal management and in their efforts to transform their relationships with other Canadian governments. The discussion then spelled out the single theme that dominates the hundreds of recommendations running through the report:

Aboriginal peoples must have room to exercise their autonomy and structure their own solutions. The pattern of debilitating and discriminatory paternalism that has characterized federal policy for the past 150 years must end. Aboriginal people cannot flourish if they are treated as wards, incapable of controlling their own destiny.[5]

In August 1995, the Government of Canada formally recognized the inherent right of self-government for Aboriginal Peoples in Canada by releasing its federal policy guide on *Aboriginal Self-Government*, which recognizes "that the Aboriginal peoples of Canada have the right to govern themselves in relation to matters that are internal to their communities, integral to their unique cultures, identities, traditions, languages and institutions, and with respect to their special relationship to their land and their resources."[6]

FOUR EXAMPLES OF SELF-GOVERNMENT ARRANGEMENTS

1. Sechelt Indian Band Self-Government Act

In 1986, BC's legislature passed the *Sechelt Indian Band Self-Government Act*,[7] providing the Sechelt Band with powers of self-government, including the power to enact its own constitution and to make laws in the areas of education, health, land use planning, local taxation, and zoning. The Sechelt Band holds fee simple (freehold ownership) title to its land, subject to limitations and conditions contained in the *Sechelt Indian Band Self-Government Act* (Sections 23–25). One of the conditions is that the band holds the lands for the use and benefit of the band and its members. It should also be noted that the enabling legislation is subject to parliamentary amendment—meaning that the Sechelt has only as much authority as Parliament delegates. Some communities regard that as a relatively weak version of self-government.

2. *Nunavut Act* and *Nunavut Land Claims Agreement Act*

In 1990, the government of the Northwest Territories and the Tunngavik Federation of Nunavut (now known as Nunavut Tunngavik Incorporated) signed an agreement-in-principle that confirmed their joint commitment to the division of the Northwest Territories (NWT) and the creation of Nunavut.[8] The formation of a new territory in the eastern NWT resulted from a double-tracked Inuit strategy: to negotiate the broadest possible comprehensive land claims agreements with the federal government and to participate actively in available political forums. Inuit members of the Legislative Assembly of the Northwest Territories collaborated with other members of legislative assemblies in preparing the 1982 plebiscite asking residents of the NWT whether they would support the creation of the new territory of Nunavut in the eastern NWT. Fifty-seven per cent of voters agreed.

3. *Nisga'a Final Agreement Act*

The Nisga'a Final Agreement[9] was signed in 1998 and came into force in April 2000. It conveyed fee simple title to two thousand square kilometres of the Nass Valley in northern BC; created separate jurisdictions within that territory for the Nisga'a Nation and the Nisga'a villages; and gave the Nisga'a Nation defined powers to co-manage hunting, fishing, and trapping rights in a much larger area (called the Nass Wildlife Area). The Nisga'a Final Agreement and the two orders of government created by that agreement are subject to the Canadian Charter of Rights and Freedoms. The Nisga'a Nation has no jurisdiction to make criminal laws.

4. Westbank First Nation Self-Government Act

With the signing of the *Westbank First Nation Self-Government Act* in 2005,[10] the Westbank First Nation became a true nation with the right to govern its own affairs and the responsibility to make decisions affecting the well-being of the community, while being held accountable to its electorate. The Westbank First Nation Government (WFNG) provides services for residents living on Westbank First Nation lands in south-central BC, including those who are non-nation members with residential leases on Westbank lands. The WFNG is one of the most progressive First Nations governments in Canada, with a comprehensive set of laws that cover items such as land use, zoning, and animal control. It provides local government services that mirror municipal services for its residents, including law enforcement, snow removal, recreation, utilities, and public works. The Act covers matrimonial and property rights, language and culture, resource management and the environment, land management, and taxes. The *Westbank First Nation Self-Government Act* also contains a provision confirming the application of the *Canadian Human Rights Act* to Westbank First Nation lands and members; the First Nation takes all necessary measures to ensure compliance of its laws and actions with Canada's international legal obligations.

Here's a snapshot of what can be included in a self-government agreement, from the Nisga'a Lisims Government summary of the Nisga'a Final Agreement:

1. Subject to age, all Nisga'a citizens may run for office and vote in Nisga'a elections;

2. Nisga'a elections must be held every five years;

3. Nisga'a Conflict of Interest guidelines and financial accountability mechanisms must be comparable to those that apply to other governments in Canada;

4. Protections to ensure standards in services, health and safety have been built into the Treaty; and,

5. Protections for non-Nisga'a residents who live on Nisga'a Lands are set out in the Treaty—this includes rights of consultation, participation and appeal where decisions of the Nisga'a Government directly and significantly affect them…[11]

As a modern treaty, the Nisga'a Final Agreement sets out and describes in detail the rights of Nisga'a citizens. Any Aboriginal rights of the Nisga'a are modified to become rights set out in the treaty. In this way, the negotiating parties have agreed to rights—rather than extinguishing them.

THE COSTS OF SELF-GOVERNMENT (AND OF THE STATUS QUO)

Everybody seems to understand that significant invest-ment will be required to make Aboriginal self-government a widespread and successful reality in Canada. Less clearly understood are the enormous and increasing costs of leav-ing things as they are. Volume 5 of the Report of the Royal Commission on Aboriginal Peoples set out a detailed analy-sis of those costs, concluding as follows:

> The political, social and economic conditions facing Aboriginal people impose a cost of [1996] $7.5 billion per year on them and on all Canadians; this cost is likely to rise in future, reaching $11 billion per year [by 2016]. This cost of the status quo includes losses flowing from failure to develop and use the full economic potential of Aboriginal people and the cost of remedial action to deal with the effects of social disintegration.[12]

What are the differences between working with a com-munity that has moved to self-government and with one that has not? The main difference is that in a self-governing community, you are working with a government that is transparent and accountable to its people rather than to the federal government. A key way to improve your Indigenous relations is to understand the governance structure within the community and the plans that may be in place to move toward a model emphasizing self-determination, self-reli-ance, and self-government.

COMMUNITY HEALING AND SELF-GOVERNMENT

Most Indigenous Peoples recognize that self-government cannot serve as a silver bullet for the deeply rooted prob-lems that plague communities.

The emphasis on personal and community healing is important because so many communities and their members suffer from the intergenerational effects of residential schools; the two go hand in hand. There is also a strong need for individuals to go through a personal healing process and then work together with other members to bring the whole community into the process. So important is this work that some communities, when offered jobs and business development opportunities from companies, have refused those opportunities and instead asked companies for help in building healing centres. There is an emerging idea that the first steps in the treaty negotiation process should be personal and focused on community healing, followed by self-government discussion and implementation, with land issues following later.

Chapter 5 described some of the key challenges that many Indigenous Peoples and communities struggle to overcome. Knowing of these issues, what can your organization do to contribute to personal and community healing?

Indigenous Relations Tips

Ask your contact within the community if any of the following would be welcome:

- Cash or services to build a healing centre
- A contribution to language revitalization programs
- Supporting cultural revival programs
- Supporting youth programs
- Contributing to the creation of a women's centre, if there is not already one in the community
- Contributing to the creation of a youth centre, if there is not already one in the community
- Contributing to the creation of a sports arena, if there is not already one in the community

{ 7 }

Isn't It True That...?
Myth vs. Reality

ΙΙΙΙΙΙΙΙΙΙΙΙΙΙΙΙΙΙΙΙΙΙΙΙΙΙΙΙΙΙΙΙΙΙΙΙΙΙΙΙΙΙΙΙΙΙΙΙΙΙΙΙΙΙΙΙΙΙΙΙΙΙ

S OME NON-INDIGENOUS PEOPLE believe that Indigenous Peoples, as defined by the *Indian Act*, receive unfair advantages. More specifically, when we talk about the *Indian Act*, we only mean status Indians as opposed to non-status Indians; Inuit and Métis do not fall under the *Indian Act* and therefore do not have the same rights, benefits, and restrictions.

While there may be some benefits for status Indians under the *Indian Act*, there are many more disadvantages. Since its proclamation in 1876, the Act has been used to:

- Replace traditional governing and decision-making systems with simple majority-elected, all-male band councils

- Ban cultural events such as the potlatch

- Limit the Indigenous land base from vast traditional territories to small reserves

- Eliminate economic development by prohibiting Indians from selling land, agricultural goods, or farm animals
- Prohibit Indians from investing moneys earned by their communities
- Prevent, until recently (1960), Indians from voting provincially or federally
- Limit the ability of Indians to leave the reserve (written permission authorized by an Indian agent was required)
- Prohibit Indians from retaining a lawyer or raising funds with the intention of hiring a lawyer
- Remove Indian children from their homes and families to attend distant government-funded and church-run Indian Residential Schools
- Eliminate diverse Indigenous identities by creating categories of "Indian-ness"—i.e., status Indians, non-status Indians, Inuit, and Métis

Many of the restrictions under the *Indian Act* violate basic human rights. Here's a little conundrum. Ask the average Canadian, "Do you support fundamental human rights as seen by the United Nations?" Most will lean toward a very strong "Yes." I think they probably view human rights as one of the things they are most proud of as Canadians. Ask the same people what they think of Aboriginal Rights, and many will lean toward "they should be equal," "they shouldn't get special treatment," and "there should be one law for everybody."

It's a conundrum because, in principle, Canadians support the idea of human rights, but practically, personally, and politically, many do not. They even, on occasion, refer to Aboriginal Rights (that is, human rights), as "special treatment" that they don't think is right, fair, or equal. But, under the *United Nations Declaration on the Rights of Indigenous Peoples*,[1] the rights of Indigenous Peoples include:

... the right to maintain and strengthen their distinct political, legal, economic, social and cultural institutions, while retaining their right to participate fully, if they so choose, in the political, economic, social and cultural life of the State.

... the right to practise and revitalize their cultural traditions and customs. This includes the right to maintain, protect and develop the past, present and future manifestations of their cultures, such as archaeological and historical sites, artefacts, designs, ceremonies, technologies and visual and performing arts and literature.

There are many myths surrounding Indigenous Peoples in Canada. We call them myths because, although they may contain an element of truth, they also miss some important information. Here we take a look at a number of the common myths and then discuss the reality for Indigenous Peoples. You will notice that I use the term "Indian"; that is because it is likely to be the term used by those who believe these myths.

Myth: "Indians already have ample reserve lands and resources."

Reality: Except for the far north (including northern Quebec), where comprehensive land claims settlements have improved the situation, the present land base of Indigenous Peoples is inadequate. Lands acknowledged as

Indigenous south of the sixtieth parallel (mainly reserves) make up 0.2 per cent of the Canadian land mass. Much of this land is of marginal value. In 2016, 339,595 Aboriginal people were living on reserve, which means 0.2 per cent of the Canadian land mass houses 20 per cent of the Aboriginal population in Canada.[2]

Myth: "Indians can do what they want with their reserve lands and resources."

Reality: The ultimate title to reserve lands is vested in the Crown. Section 29 of the *Indian Act* states, "Reserve lands are not subject to seizure under legal process."

The *Indian Act* is clear that status Indians do not own property on reserves. CIRNAC may issue a Certificate of Possession to a status Indian for a portion of reserve land, but underlying title to the land remains vested with the Crown. Thus, Indian reserve land cannot be sold except to the Crown and does not appreciate in value the same way that property held in fee simple (freehold ownership) does for other Canadians. This makes it very difficult for a status Indian to borrow funds to build a house—or start a business—on-reserve.

Myth: "Indians get free housing."

Reality: Indigenous Peoples can apply for social housing programs offered by the Canada Mortgage and Housing Corporation (CMHC). CMHC offers many programs to assist Indigenous and non-Indigenous people in meeting their housing needs. The programs for Indigenous Peoples are mainly designed to give low-income families access to rental housing. First Nations that meet CMHC lending criteria apply to a bank for conventional mortgage funds to finance the social housing construction, usually with CMHC providing loan insurance.

Myth: "Indians don't pay taxes."

Reality: This misconception is proclaimed frequently. Federal tax exemptions for status Indians have existed at least since the consolidation of the *Indian Act* in 1876 but only apply in very specific and limited conditions. Under Sections 87 and 90 of the *Indian Act*, status Indians do not pay federal or provincial taxes on their personal and real property that is on a reserve. Personal property includes goods, services, and income as defined under Canada Revenue Agency policies. As income is considered personal property, status Indians who work on a reserve do not pay federal or provincial taxes on their employment income. However, income earned by Inuit and Métis is not eligible for this exemption. Inuit and Métis generally do not live on reserves, and income earned by status Indians off-reserve is taxable. The Supreme Court of Canada has concluded that the purpose of this exemption is to preserve the entitlements of status Indians to their reserve lands and to ensure that the use of their property on their reserve lands is not eroded by taxes.

Section 87 also exempts from the federal Goods and Services Tax (GST) the goods and services bought by status Indians at businesses located on-reserve. Goods and services purchased off-reserve by status Indians but delivered to the reserve are also tax exempt. Most provincial sales taxes are similarly applied. In some provinces, there are certain exemptions such as automobiles, which must be registered to an address on a reserve in order to be tax exempt.

Again, it's a myth that Indigenous Peoples don't pay tax. Really it is only status Indians who can qualify for exemptions under Section 87. Inuit, Métis, and non-status Indians are under the same tax regime as other taxpayers in Canada

Myth: "Indians get free post-secondary education."

Reality: To say that all Indigenous Peoples receive free post-secondary funding is misleading because it implies that all Indigenous Peoples are eligible for funding. Only status Indians are eligible to receive funding for post-secondary education through Indigenous Services Canada. Post-secondary education funding is part of the legal and constitutional obligation of the federal government.

In order to create additional opportunities for their members, some bands set aside funding within their budgets to assist their members in obtaining a post-secondary education. These programs are similar to scholarship programs established by post-secondary institutions and other organizations that want to see the advancement of youth. But it means they may have to take badly needed funds from housing, infrastructure, health budgets, and so on.

While in some communities the rate of high school graduation is increasing, graduates often step off the path to higher education at that point due to the lack of available funds. If they live off-reserve, they are often not eligible to receive funding.

Myth: "Indians have special rights."

Reality: The myth of "special rights" is frequently proclaimed in relation to fishing, hunting, and gathering rights. Aboriginal Peoples fight long and expensive legal battles to defend their legal rights that were included in the *Constitution Act, 1982*, under Section 35:

(1) The existing aboriginal and treaty rights of the aboriginal people in Canada are hereby recognized and affirmed.

(2) In this Act, "aboriginal peoples of Canada" includes the Indian, Inuit and Métis peoples of Canada.

(3) For greater certainty, in subsection (1), "treaty rights" includes rights that now exist by way of land claims agreements or may be so acquired.

(4) Notwithstanding any other provision of this Act, the aboriginal and treaty rights referred to in subsection (1) are guaranteed equally to male and female persons.

Section 35 neither confirms nor creates absolute Aboriginal Rights. It does confirm "existing aboriginal or treaty rights" that had not been extinguished by surrender or legislation before 1982.

On the other hand, Aboriginal Rights and Treaty Rights existing after the proclamation of the *Constitution Act, 1982*, now receive significant legal protection under Section 35.

Aboriginal Rights are collectively held and include:

- Rights to the land (Aboriginal Title)
- Rights to subsistence resources and activities (hunting, fishing, gathering)
- The right to self-determination and self-government
- The right to practise one's own culture and customs including language and religion, sometimes referred to as the right of "cultural integrity"
- The right to enter into treaties[3]

Individual nations can have specific rights which may be in treaties or have been won in a court case. An example is the Musqueam Band which, as a result of the *Sparrow* decision in 1990, have the legal right to fish.

It should be noted that Aboriginal Rights are synonymous with human rights and that Canada and Canadians have long valued the human rights of peoples around the world and at home.

Myth: "Residential schools are ancient history, so why can't they just get over it."

Reality: Residential schools are not "ancient history." It may seem as though they belong to a dim past, due to the horrific conditions the 150,000 children (of whom 6,000 died or disappeared) were subjected to, but the last one closed in 1996. That's not ancient history.

The mandate of the schools was to assimilate the children into settler society. The actions taken to fulfill the mandate of assimilation have been labelled "cultural genocide" by leading political and legal minds, including former chief justice Beverley McLachlin, former prime minister Paul Martin, and Senator Murray Sinclair.

"Genocide" is not a term that most people associate with Canada. What constitutes genocide? Article II of the United Nations Genocide Convention[4] contains a narrow definition of the crime of genocide, which includes two main elements:

1. *A mental element:* the "intent to destroy, in whole or in part, a national, ethnical, racial or religious group, as such."

2. *A physical element*, which includes the following five acts, enumerated exhaustively:
   - Killing members of the group
   - Causing serious bodily or mental harm to members of the group
   - Deliberately inflicting on the group conditions of life calculated to bring about its physical destruction in whole or in part
   - Imposing measures intended to prevent births within the group
   - Forcibly transferring children of the group to another group

Children as young as six were forcibly removed from their homes and sent to residential schools. From the moment they crossed the threshold of the school, they were thrust into a harsh, unforgiving, linguistically and culturally alien world. Punishment was often severe, with sexual, physical, and psychological abuse common. The legacy of the trauma those children suffered is carried forth through the generations.

A frequent extension of the "residential schools are ancient history" myth is the question "Why can't they just get over it?" Senator Murray Sinclair, former head of the Truth and Reconciliation Commission of Canada, made these comments regarding a fellow senator who posed that question:

> My answer has always been: why can't you always remember this? Because this is about memorializing

those people who have been the victims of a great wrong. Why don't you tell the United States to "get over" 9/11? Why don't you tell this country to "get over" all the veterans who died in the Second World War, instead of honouring them once a year?... We should never forget, even once we have learned from it, because it's part of who we are. It's not just a part of who we are as survivors and children of survivors and relatives of survivors; it's part of who we are as a nation. And this nation must never forget what it once did to its most vulnerable people.[5]

By knowing the facts, and not being afraid to speak up, you can help turn the tide on the continued existence of these myths.

Indigenous Relations Tips

- If you hear something that sounds like a myth or stereotype, don't be polite and let it slide. Simply ask, "Are you sure you have that right?"
- Educate yourself on the facts.
- Share our free ebook on myths: *Dispelling Common Myths About Indigenous Peoples* with family, friends, and colleagues (available on ictinc.ca under the Free tab).

NOW THAT YOU have the background on some of the primary issues facing Indigenous Peoples, it's time to delve into how to incorporate that understanding into your relationships with Indigenous people and communities.

As an Indigenous relations trainer, I saw a need for a model, or a list of actions, our clients could follow to assist them in their goal to work respectfully and effectively with Indigenous Peoples and communities.

Cindy and I developed and field tested the RESPECT model, which I teach in my Working Effectively with Indigenous Peoples® and Indigenous Relations courses. I've now taught it to thousands of people who take our training for personal and professional fulfillment. I'm sharing it with you here, along with additional tips and suggestions to guide you on your journey.

RESPECT: A Path toward Working Effectively with Indigenous Peoples®

||||||||||||||||||||||||||||||||||||||||||||||||||||||||||||||||||||||||||||||||||||||||||

HOW DOES ONE work effectively with Indigenous Peoples? Is there one process you can use that will work in every situation? The short answer is "No." The appropriate process in any given situation will change depending on the communities involved and on the various policies and legal, cultural, and regional considerations on the table.

Prominent national Indigenous leaders have commented that any effective Indigenous relations process should be designed to address the three Rs—Recognition, Respect, and Reconciliation.

Recognition means to recognize constitutionally protected Aboriginal Rights.

Respect means to address the uniqueness of individual Indigenous Peoples, their cultures, and their constitutionally protected rights.

Reconciliation means to restore harmony between Indigenous and non-Indigenous people.

From the concept of the three Rs, we developed a training model called RESPECT, which is designed to provide guidance to individuals and organizations seeking to build effective relationships with Indigenous Peoples.

RESPECT stands for:

Research
Examine
Strategize
Present
Evaluate
Customize
Transform

The visual model below depicts RESPECT as a continuous process of learning, developing, and evolving. We present RESPECT not as a firm protocol for behaviour but rather as a principled approach to relationship building, which we see as the key to working effectively with Indigenous communities.

Research

A critical component of working effectively with Indigenous communities is research. No successful international business person would go to another country to do business without researching legal and cultural differences and considering their impact on existing business processes and practices. That business person would undertake the research in-house so that in meetings they

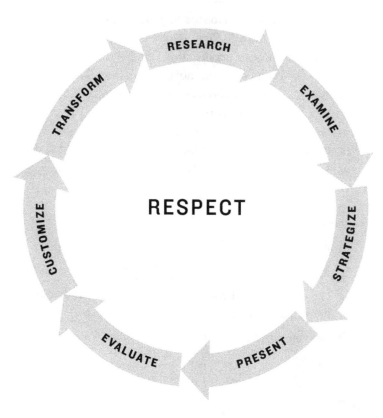

are aware, up to speed, and respectful. It's unlikely they would just ask their potential partner to "fill them in." So, why wouldn't you research the nation you're consulting with or the community you're visiting? It's not up to the community to educate you.

ASSESSING YOUR ORGANIZATION

Research is not limited to studying the community—start by researching within. First, determine where you, your colleagues, and your organization stand on working with Indigenous Peoples and on Indigenous issues. Before you apply a relationship-building strategy, conduct the following assessment to determine your organization's level of understanding and support. Then you will have a sense of the amount and focus of internal work required before your organization embarks on a plan to build an effective working relationship.

You:

❑ Are you comfortable working with Indigenous Peoples?

❑ Are you comfortable engaging with Indigenous issues?

❑ Have you worked with Indigenous Peoples and communities in the past?

❑ Are you currently working with Indigenous Peoples and communities?

❑ Overall, would you like to see Indigenous land claims resolved sooner rather than later?

❑ Do you support a municipal model of Indigenous self-government?

❑ Do you support a model of self-government that includes broader powers?

❑ Do you have personal contacts for Indigenous advice?

❑ Do you have time to learn about Indigenous Peoples and Indigenous issues?

❑ Are you willing to give up other activities to make time for Indigenous learning?

Your colleagues:

❑ Are your colleagues comfortable working with Indigenous Peoples?

❑ Are they comfortable engaging with Indigenous issues?

❑ Have they worked with Indigenous communities in the past?

❑ Are they currently working with Indigenous communities?

❑ Overall, would they like to see land claims resolved sooner rather than later?

❑ Do they support a municipal model of self-government?

❑ Do they support a model of self-government that includes broader powers?

❑ Do they believe Indigenous Peoples have "special" fishing and hunting rights or that they receive "special treatment"?

❑ Do they have time to learn about Indigenous Peoples and Indigenous issues?

❑ Are they willing to give up other activities to make time for Indigenous learning?

Your organization:

❑ Is your organization comfortable working with Indigenous Peoples?

❑ Is your organization comfortable engaging with Indigenous issues?

❑ Has your organization worked with Indigenous communities in the past?

❑ Is your organization currently working with Indigenous communities?

❑ Does your organization publicly support the practice of respect, recognition, and reconciliation of constitutionally protected Aboriginal Rights?

❑ Does your organization publicly support the inherent right of Indigenous self-government?

❑ Will your organization commit time to learning about Indigenous Peoples and Indigenous issues?

❑ Is your organization willing to give up other activities to make time for Indigenous learning?

❑ Can your organization "do what it takes" to get the job done?

❑ Will your organization commit funds to capacity-building for Indigenous Peoples?

❑ Does your organization have a formal Indigenous relations policy? If so, will that policy give you leverage when working internally to promote Indigenous relations?

❑ Can and will your organization extend timelines to accommodate working with Indigenous Peoples?

❑ Does your organization understand that its objectives and Indigenous community objectives won't always mesh?

LEARNING ABOUT THE INDIGENOUS COMMUNITY

You also need to conduct research on the Indigenous Peoples with whom you may develop a relationship. Ideally, that research should be performed before you and your organization begin working in the community. But better late than never!

⁣⁣

Be aware of significant events that can compromise your ability to engage people or communities in relationship building.

⁣⁣

The following checklists will start you in your research.

Cultural background information:

- ❑ Community cultural centres
- ❑ Provincial museums
- ❑ Books on communities
- ❑ Books by community authors
- ❑ Traditional use studies
- ❑ Government websites (federal and provincial)
- ❑ Community websites
- ❑ Other public submissions (for example, regulatory submissions)

People you should consider talking to:

- ❏ Government representatives who have worked with the community or communities in question—federal and provincial at a minimum
- ❏ Consultants
- ❏ Lawyers
- ❏ Economic development officers
- ❏ Contacts from the specific Indigenous community/ies

Information to look for:

- ❏ Community profiles and statistics
- ❏ Fishing, hunting, and gathering activities
- ❏ Spiritual practices
- ❏ Custom, elected, or majority-elected leadership
- ❏ Tribal council or treaty offices affiliations
- ❏ Other political affiliations (e.g., Assembly of First Nations)
- ❏ Decision-making structures
- ❏ Staff directories
- ❏ Community priorities
- ❏ Date of the next band election
- ❏ Questions they will ask you
- ❏ Media stories outlining main issues
- ❏ Past agreements—written or verbal
- ❏ Role of hereditary leaders and elders
- ❏ *Indian Act* legislation that pertains to your work

STAYING UP-TO-DATE ON INDIGENOUS ISSUES

A key to working effectively with Indigenous communities is to try to understand their perspectives in advance. Learning a community's history and current issues will enable you to anticipate their priorities and core concerns about your business interests. To do this, you can follow these steps:

- Bookmark our blog *Working Effectively with Indigenous Peoples®* (ictinc.ca/blog), which posts new articles weekly on a wide range of topics

- Sign up for the blog's free newsletter, *Indigenous Relations Bulletin*, which provides a monthly roundup of articles (ictinc.ca/newsletter-sign-up)

- Read the Report of the Royal Commission on Aboriginal Peoples

- Read the Truth and Reconciliation Commission's Final Report and associated 94 Calls to Action (available online and in *21 Things You May Not Know About the Indian Act*)

- Read books on communities and related issues

- Check out the websites of Indigenous organizations

- Subscribe to Indigenous media and newsletters

- Follow Indigenous thought leaders and community leaders on social media

Google Alerts

Take advantage of free services such as Google Alerts, which lets you track any issue, community, or person by monitoring the web for specific terms that you want to be alerted on. Pick a term, like "Mi'kmaq," for example, and Google will monitor the web for new occurrences of the term. You can specify whether you want to receive reports daily, weekly, or monthly.

Examine

The next step in the RESPECT process is to examine the information compiled to date—particularly, the potential impact of the community's key issues on your work, and the impact of your work on the community. Let's discuss issues that can have an impact on operations and some suggestions for addressing them.

TIMING IS EVERYTHING

Timing can be everything for the person who is looking to build relationships with an Indigenous community. Consider nations whose cultures revolve around fish and fishing. Those nations have a very limited window (dictated by nature and regulated by the Department of Fisheries and Oceans) in which to catch enough fish to feed their members through the winter. The priority of fishing can extend to the entire community—including the chief and council. In this environment, it may be next to impossible to get a meeting together during the fishing season.

Or you may be trying to talk to a community about scheduling activities such as pesticide application or tree thinning. Suppose that you get resistance and then, with some good dialogue, you determine that the community wants to pick berries in your proposed work area at that time of the year. Would you consider changing your plans to make way for their berry picking? It could mean the difference between deepening resistance and broadening consensus.

Next, consider the issue of death in an Indigenous community. Life is precious in any community, but population is a critical concern to communities struggling to grow as nations. It is not uncommon for all of the nation's operations, including the band office, to shut down completely following a death. If this happens, extend your condolences to the community and wait at least ten days before contacting them to schedule another time to meet.

You may want to call ahead to confirm your scheduled meeting, and if you are travelling a great distance, you may be wise to confirm again while in transit.

"YOU KNOW WHAT HAPPENS WHEN YOU ASSUME"

The following examples highlight the importance of conducting thorough research. With knowledge you will gain from this book coupled with information available on the internet, there is no legitimate reason for someone to make these mistakes when working with Indigenous communities. These examples also highlight the need for cultural competency training; these types of rookie errors can be avoided.

Example 1: Why didn't you return my call?

Fred was tasked by his organization to consult with First Nations on a permit application. He took a look at the map and noticed a reserve in the approximate permit application area. Fred went online and attempted to contact the band to engage them in consultation. After repeated attempts, he was finally able to reach someone in the band office. He was a little annoyed by the time he got through, and his irritation was apparent in his discussion with the nation's representative. "I wanted to consult with you. Why didn't you return my call?" The reply was that this was not the traditional territory of the nation Fred had contacted. He needed to contact a different nation.

Fred could have avoided the embarrassment and the unnecessary delay if he had been more thorough in his research and learned the history of the Indigenous Peoples in the region. When Indian agents were designating reserve land, the location was not necessarily anywhere near the nation's traditional land.

Example 2: A short-lived consensus

George was asked by his organization to deliver a community presentation on an upcoming project. In his research, he identified a nation with a hyphenated name, whose office was located in the area the project would traverse. After several meetings with the nation, George began to get community consensus on preferred routing and terms of accommodation. But upon review with others in his organization, George learned that there was a problem and that the consensus might be short-lived. The nation's band council was made up of representatives from the second nation of the hyphenated name: they had been amalgamated with the nation of the first name. The project was going to pass through the traditional territory of the first-named nation of the amalgamated nation.

George may have assumed that since the bands shared a name, they shared a territory, which is not always the case. George should have conducted some research into why the nations were joined together in a hyphenated name and learned about the individual histories of each of the nations prior to amalgamation. It may be that one nation cannot speak for another nation.

Example 3: Joint initiative

Wendy, a new employee with the city, was called into a meeting to discuss a recent incident that some members of the media had branded as racism and others had dismissed as an unfortunate set of circumstances. The incident was still fresh in the minds of the local Indigenous community and the city wanted to address it. Wendy suggested an approach to the local Friendship Centre. The city moved forward with the idea, and Wendy contacted the Friendship Centre to seek their support for a joint initiative. They agreed to sign an accord at a public event to address the issue and make things better in the future. On the day of the signing, a local nation came forward to protest their exclusion from the accord, noting that one of their members was involved in the original incident. Which group was most affected by the event? If the incident had involved a Friendship Centre patron, it would have made sense to work with the Friendship Centre to resolve it. However, this situation should have been resolved with the local nation.

Wendy would have been wise to contact the person affected by the incident and then work with that person's nation to plan the initiative and organize the accord-signing event. Wendy may not have been comfortable contacting the nation or even aware that she should contact them but, nonetheless, she should have considered doing so. This is a situation in which some Indigenous awareness training would have provided Wendy with a comfort level for her communications with Indigenous Peoples.

Strategize

COMMUNITY ENGAGEMENT STRATEGY

With the initial research and examination complete, it's time to put together a strategy for approaching the community that you hope to engage with. Consider both individual and organizational approaches to the community's cultural and political issues, planning your verbal and nonverbal communications with care. Here are some considerations for an effective community engagement strategy.

Create a formal in-house Indigenous Policy:

❑ Ensure there is a solid understanding of the need for Indigenous relations

❑ Dedicate appropriate staff to form a project team

❑ Provide training for project team members

❑ Ensure Indigenous awareness training is provided for all staff/managers

❑ Ensure staff and financial resources are available to implement the policy over the long-term

❑ Ensure there is support in the upper levels of management

❑ Work with local Indigenous leaders and communities to further develop the policy

❑ Incorporate the Indigenous Policy into your organization's mandate

❑ Communicate the policy to all employees

❑ Post the policy on your organization's website and other materials

❑ Set and post goals, and appoint staff to realize goals

❑ Develop an accountability process

❑ Develop a system for monitoring progress of goals

❑ Communicate progress of the policy program throughout the organization

❑ Consider enrolling your organization in the Progressive Aboriginal Relations (PAR) program of the Canadian Council for Aboriginal Business

Create a formal Community Relations Policy:

❑ Work with the community/ies to establish a community liaison committee

❑ Assist the community liaison committee with their outreach efforts to contact everyone in the community, whether on- or off-reserve

❑ Appoint staff to work with the community liaison committee

❑ Include reports/issues/concerns from the community liaison committee in internal company newsletters

Create a formal Community Development Policy:

- ❏ Work with communities to identify their community development needs
- ❏ Work with communities to develop an economic development strategy
- ❏ Allocate funding for community infrastructure
- ❏ Support and, if invited, attend community events

CULTURAL SURVIVAL

The name of the game for Indigenous Peoples everywhere is cultural survival. Every decision an Indigenous community makes reflects this value; that's why decisions can take longer in Indigenous communities.

The Seventh Generation Principle says that all decisions must include consideration of impacts on community members seven generations into the future. This principle is reflected in Indigenous thinking throughout North America and around the globe.

How might the Seventh Generation Principle affect your community interaction?

First, you may have two different perspectives of time (review the discussion of worldviews in chapter 4). For most companies, the operational time frame is driven by quarterly reports and fiscal year-ends. In Indigenous communities, the time frame is much, much longer.

Second, cultural survival makes Indigenous Peoples do things that may not immediately make sense from a business perspective. For example, suppose that a large resource company offers a billion dollars to an Indigenous community for access to their ancestral land. The community refuses outright. The organization is flabbergasted and states that it is another example of Indigenous irrationality or shortsightedness. But in the context of cultural survival, the decision makes sense. Some First Nations sold their lands for "beads and baubles" in centuries past. Those agreements were ill equipped to deal with today's environment and have led to almost insurmountable challenges. Today's nations will consider cultural survival very seriously when making decisions involving their ancestral land. As an example, an offshore LNG proponent wanted to build a plant on an island in the territory of a First Nation on the West Coast. The proponent's offer was rejected because of its impact on salmon fry habitat. That piece of the project plan had to be reworked before they could reach an agreement.

SACRED LANDS

Buffalo jumps, sweat lodges, bathing pools, whaling shrines, transformation rocks, first ancestor sites, petroglyphs, spirit dancing, burial grounds, ceremony sites, and birthing spots on the land are just a few examples of sacred sites in Indigenous cultures. If your proposed activity encroaches on such an area, you may encounter fierce resistance from local communities. Your main challenge will be to get them even to talk about such sites. Depending on the significance of the site and the degree of trust you have already earned with the community, you could experience anything from the cold shoulder to blockades and legal action. Some communities will go to extremes to protect their sacred sites. The 1995 Ipperwash Crisis and the 1990 Oka Crisis are two examples of Indigenous

Peoples protecting sacred lands. Patience will be required in building the trust needed to get discussion underway.

If you encounter resistance such as the cold shoulder, consider asking, "Is there something here that you cannot discuss because it is sacred to the community? If so, I would be happy to agree to not disclose it to the public."

CONNECTIVITY PRINCIPLE

The worldviews of many Indigenous Peoples include a principle of connectivity. In this view, everything is connected. The spirit world is connected to the mortal world, the sea is connected to the land, the sky is connected to the ground, and so on.

It's common for non-Indigenous people to try to isolate certain issues in framing their discussions with an Indigenous community. For example, you think your project will only affect this part of the county, cut block (a clearing for forestry), or valley, and so you frame it as such.

The Indigenous community, in contrast, will likely not consider any issue in isolation, and they likely won't call it a "valley"—Indigenous Peoples will think "territory." Before deciding on an issue, they will think about that cut block plus all the other cut blocks in their territory, and the cumulative effects of oil and gas, mining, and logging operations on hunting and fishing throughout the territory.

URBAN VS. RURAL NATIONS

There can be big differences between nations located in urban areas and nations that are in more rural areas. Dress codes, timeliness of meetings, and so on will vary. If you are working with both urban and rural nations, you will have to shift gears as you move from nation to nation. You may also have to consider that there can be significant issues and differences between a nation's reserve residents and its urban members. Some nations work closely with their urban members, while others do not.

For ratification of big agreements, you need the support of all community members, as the rights of Indigenous Peoples are held by a collective and not just the people living on-reserve. Some nations, to ensure there is broad support for their work, have held referendums that included both on-reserve members and those who have relocated. Some communities may not reach out to off-reserve members; that could be at their peril and yours, if it's your project.

What do you do if the leadership is not interested in garnering support from all community members, regardless of their location? Be concerned that they don't want to tell anyone in the community what's going on. Try to find tactful ways to get further community engagement. We have seen examples in which the community was unaware of what was going on and then, once they found out, worked very hard to stop the project.

YOUR TIMELINE IS YOUR PROBLEM

Timelines are thorny issues in Indigenous communities. At present, almost everyone who goes to a community to do business comes with a timeline. Do you really want to add yourself to that list? You will likely win respect and a more receptive audience if you approach the community with an attitude marked by interest and willingness to listen, leaving your timeline back in the office. If, however, you set a rigid timeline before engaging with the community, you may find the issues are more complex than you anticipated. If the unexpected issues are not handled correctly, you can open yourself up to risks such as legal challenges and judicial reviews, negative media campaigns, and direct action and resistance, which can add years to your timeline. Any or all of these activities can be costly in terms of financial consideration and could result in no final investment decision.

For example, look at the 2016–2017 Dakota Access Pipeline (DAPL) controversy as an example of the financial and social impact of pushing hard on a timeline. The financial and social costs accrued by firms with an ownership stake in the pipeline, by the banks that financed it, and by governments during the blockade are staggering. Here are some ways it could have unfolded differently:

- Do thorough research on social risks related to human rights, especially those associated with Indigenous Peoples.

- Disclose social risks so that investors have a clear view of total risks inherent in a development project.

- Understand that social costs affect not only the share value of investors but also local communities, states, taxpayers, and Indigenous governments. Local communities often bear the financial burden when companies fail to obtain consent from Indigenous Peoples regarding projects that impact them. And these communities often have the fewest resources.

- Respect that social movements today frequently gain audiences and support around the world.

Now apply the DAPL pipeline scenario to Canada. Had the community consultation been managed through the lens of the *United Nations Declaration on the Rights of Indigenous Peoples*, it likely would have unfolded quite differently.

UNDRIP is an international declaration that sets out "the minimum standards for the survival, dignity, and well-being of Indigenous Peoples of the world" (article 43). It is a legally non-binding document that outlines norms and principles to guide state interactions with Indigenous Peoples. The forty-six articles include recognition of the rights of Indigenous Peoples to self-determination, equality, protection of their respective cultures, a collective identity, and economic and social development.

Honouring UNDRIP is where the future of consultation (and reconciliation) with Indigenous Peoples is headed. The Truth and Reconciliation Commission's 94 Calls to Actions include these:

43. We call upon federal, provincial, territorial, and municipal governments to fully adopt and implement the *United Nations Declaration on the Rights of Indigenous Peoples* as the framework for reconciliation.

44. We call upon the Government of Canada to develop a national action plan, strategies, and other concrete measures to achieve the goals of the *United Nations Declaration on the Rights of Indigenous Peoples*.

In May 2016, when Canada removed the official objector status that the country had maintained for six years and endorsed UNDRIP, it sparked reactions ranging from joy and empowerment to fear, gloom, doubt, and confusion. The crux of the confusion over UNDRIP is the question "Veto or no veto?" The Crown's existing "duty to consult" with Indigenous Peoples on issues that might affect their interests is constitutionally protected but does not confer a veto.

UNDRIP, on the other hand, uses a standard of consultation that calls upon governments to obtain "free, prior and informed consent" (FPIC) from Indigenous Peoples on issues that might affect their interests. So, in an UNDRIP context, it is no longer good enough to simply meet the guidelines and principles of Indigenous consultation; the Crown and project proponents would now have to ensure that FPIC has been obtained if they are seeking economic certainty.

So what should a developer do in such a situation with moving targets? The answer will depend on the developer, but we have always said that it is better to get consent from a community for your project than it is not to have it. If you gain consent ahead of time, you avoid having your project stalled by legal battles. We have noticed that firms with Impact and Benefit Agreements, or IBAs (a contract that says there will be impacts on rights but there will be benefits in exchange—a consent of sorts), tend to do better than developers without such agreements.

Also, the long-term trend of consultation and legal direction from the courts with respect to Indigenous Peoples has gone from mere consultation in the early rounds of the *Delgamuukw and Gisday'way* lower-level court decisions in the mid-1990s,[1] to beyond more consultation, and could go up to full consent of the nations whose lands are at stake. In summary, the best way to ensure a project will be built is to have consent of some sort. Anything less than consent can open avenues of legal challenges, negative media campaigns, and project delays.

One good way to deal with timeline issues is to have project managers build additional time into business planning processes and policies to accommodate the Indigenous community. Another is to provide capacity funding.

Capacity funding is a cost-efficient measure in which you provide funding to the community, so they can hire experts to review permit applications, environmental assessments, project proposals, and so on, on their behalf. This adds some predictability to when your reports and permit requests will be completed, which means your company can at least tentatively schedule the work into project timeline and budgets.

In some Indigenous communities, staff are fully occupied with looking after community needs. They frequently do not have time or expertise to review technical reports and permit applications or the resources to hire someone to review them on their behalf. A prime example is the immensity of the technical report the Squamish Nation was expected to review as part of the National Energy Board's hearings on the proposed Trans Mountain pipeline system expansion. According to the judge's ruling on the process:

> Chief Campbell of the Squamish Nation provided evidence that the funding provided to Squamish was not adequate for Squamish to obtain experts to review and respond **to the 8 volume, 15,000 page, highly technical Project application.** Nor, in his view, was the funding adequate for Squamish to undertake a comprehensive assessment of the impacts of the Project on Squamish rights and title. He notes that Squamish's limited budget is fully subscribed to meet the needs of its members and that the sole purpose of Squamish's involvement in the hearing and consultation process was "defensive: to protect our rights and title."[2] [emphasis added]

WATCH OUT

I was told a funny story by a community leader about a person who really wanted to work with the community. The person spent a long time trying to get a meeting and was finally successful. The meeting was to take place in a remote fly-in community. The main issue was that the visitor had an annoying habit of checking his watch. He was, of course, worried about the return flight, which he did not want to miss. It got so bad that the community members started to filibuster the follow-up meetings just to see how long they could keep the visitor sitting there.

|||||||||||||||||||||||||||||||||||||||||||||||||||||||||||||||||||||||||||||||||||||||||||||||||||||||||||||||||||||||||||||||||||||||||||||||||||||||||||||||

Avoid annoying habits such as checking your watch; be present in your conversations.

|||||||||||||||||||||||||||||||||||||||||||||||||||||||||||||||||||||||||||||||||||||||||||||||||||||||||||||||||||||||||||||||||||||||||||||||||||||||||||||||

A PLACE ON THE AGENDA

Many chiefs, councils, and administrators don't meet every day or even every week; instead, they meet periodically and try to cover many agenda items in a single sitting. If you want to make a presentation at the next council meeting, try to find a good place on the agenda. By a "good place," I mean you don't want to follow a presentation that is likely to be contentious, as those emotions will likely spill over onto you and your presentation.

One suggestion is to ask for a copy of the agenda in advance of the meeting. If your position on it is unfavourable, then ask for a better position or maybe even be prepared to postpone your presentation until the next council meeting where you might get better placement. Also, be aware that with many items on an agenda, you are unlikely to get all the time you are asking for. You may have to reduce your presentation significantly.

AUTHORITY FIGURES AND THE LEGACY OF RESIDENTIAL SCHOOLS

A difficult issue that may influence your relationship with Indigenous Peoples is that of residential schools and authority figures. Many of the people you will be working with attended residential schools—segregated from their families and cultures, possibly subjected to physical and sexual abuse, and almost certainly traumatized by their experiences; many refer to themselves as "survivors." They still have bitter memories associated with those schools, and the effects are intergenerational. Be aware that these survivors may have issues with authority figures and that, depending on the role you have in communicating with the community, you might represent authority.

If someone raises residential school issues with you, listen carefully and respectfully. Don't get defensive and don't take it personally—and definitely don't absolve yourself of personal responsibility by saying, "I wasn't there" or "I had nothing to do with it." Instead, be prepared to acknowledge the issue by saying something along the lines of "Thank you for sharing your experiences of residential schools and their impact on you personally, on your family, and on the community. It helps me understand the impact and shows me the importance of the formal apology, baseline compensation, and the Truth and Reconciliation Commission recommendations. I'm hoping that my work with the community will somehow contribute to reconciliation."

As part of your strategy, choose carefully the people who will work with the community. Avoid sending anyone who has an authoritative attitude, has a brusque manner, shows impatience, or speaks and moves quickly.

GENDER

In chapter 2, we discussed the rich variety of traditional social structures of Indigenous Peoples in Canada. In patrilineal communities, where the passage of power and authority goes through the men, men occupy centre stage and are the traditional leaders. In matrilineal communities, the passage of power goes down through the women; women occupy centre stage and are the traditional leaders. In still other communities, men carry out leadership and administrative roles delegated to them by powerful women who remain in the background.

We have noted the importance of identifying the leadership structures and assessing the governance traditions that apply to the particular community in question. Determining the role of gender in decision-making is a vital part of that assessment. Matching your team to the community's cultural norms is a good strategy that can help improve working relationships. Conversely, not matching can hinder your progress. I once had the privilege of learning this lesson first-hand. A male colleague had been working on a project with a particular Indigenous community. The decision-making structure was led by a female member of this community. By chance, on a later visit to the community, we asked the chief, "How is it going with that project?" She replied, "You know how we work here ... and look who you sent to work with us."

Try to match your team's composition with the community's decision-making structure. If women are the decision makers, then send women. Or, as my mother-in-law would say in that situation, "If you're gonna send a man, at least send a sexy one."

NAME DROPPING

To name drop or not to name drop, that is the question. In this era of incessant, high-octane networking, name dropping can become just part of the conversation—associations with people who are considered influential are used as leverage to open doors. But in some cases, it is inappropriate, particularly in building relationships with Indigenous communities. Depending on the situation and the name you are using, name dropping can be perceived as intimidation. The very people you are trying to impress may pay more attention to the fact that you are name dropping than they do to the name you are dropping— the intended "wow" factor may be completely ignored.

Here are three situations where name dropping can be problematic when working with Indigenous Peoples.

1. **Communities:** Say you are working with a number of communities in your effort to build consensus for your project. You have the opportunity to meet the chief and council. Thinking it will help your case if you indicate that other communities are on board, you say something like, "I was just at such-and-such community and they loved my presentation and can't wait for us to get started." Communities, like people, have relationships and can be in conflict. Unless you are sure that there is a respectful relationship between the two communities, avoid saying which other communities you have visited unless you are asked. As part of the due diligence that you do before meeting with community members, learn the history of the area and what the relationships are like between communities.

2. **Personalities:** It is difficult to know how any one person may view a "big name," so it's better to avoid name dropping altogether when becoming acquainted with Indigenous communities. Don't assume an Indigenous celebrity or person of renown is unequivocally and universally respected—that's one of those nasty assumptions.

3. **Individuals:** Name dropping to individuals is of little value to the relationship. Again, don't assume that if people have something in common, they would automatically know and respect the same people and share common outlooks. And you don't ever want to say, "Some of my best friends are Native, First Nations, Inuit, or Indigenous," as a way of trying to make yourself look good.

There is no question that name dropping can be helpful in the right circumstances, but in the wrong circumstances it can have detrimental effects. Do the research beforehand to ensure you are safe.

||||||||||||||||||||||||||||||||||||||||||||||||||||||||||||||||||||||||||||||||||||||||||||||||||||||||||||||||||||||

Before name dropping, be sure to see if the person belongs to the same tribal council or treaty council as the community you are working with. Additional research into the relationships between member tribal or treaty councils should show whether there are visible signs of internal conflict between individual communities.

||||||||||||||||||||||||||||||||||||||||||||||||||||||||||||||||||||||||||||||||||||||||||||||||||||||||||||||||||||||

PEOPLE ALIGNMENT

The old saying "You can tell a lot about people by the company they keep" will apply to your work in Indigenous communities. For example, if there is an upcoming election and you have aligned yourself with the outgoing chief or council, you may have created a serious people alignment problem for your project.

Your selection of consultants to work on your behalf can require similar sensitivity. The reputation of how your hired consultant works with Indigenous Peoples will be considered a reflection on you and your company—so hire accordingly.

When attending a multi-party meeting with an Indigenous community, try not to sit close to people whose issues with the community are more contentious than yours, as you could inadvertently be perceived as part of that contentious issue.

DRESSING APPROPRIATELY

If you show up for work in an Indigenous community wearing high heels with lots of makeup and jewelry, or a three-piece suit complete with paisley tie and dress shoes, it can send the wrong messages. The first message is that you have lots of money to spend. The second is that you're a "defender of the empire." Both messages can have serious ramifications for your upcoming meeting, and they set a tone that may not accurately reflect you or your organization.

Generally speaking, the dress standard in Indigenous communities is quite casual. For both men and women, jeans and casual shirts are usually the norm. Always take your lead from community representatives—if they wear shirts and ties or business suits, then by all means dress accordingly. If your dress code at work requires business attire, then try to plan your schedule so you can show up at community meetings dressed more casually; at the very least, you can remove the jacket, tie, and jewelry beforehand. It is also a good idea to wear "weather ready" clothing and footgear. If you are going to wear Indigenous jewelry, try to choose designs from the community you are working in.

GIFTS: TO GIVE OR RECEIVE?

People often ask if they should bring gifts to meetings and other community events. In some cases, it may be appropriate and even expected; in others, it can actually be offensive—even coming across as a bribe. So, how can you know when to bring a gift and what kind of gift is appropriate? The key is simply to ask the host or the administrative person who is helping to set up the meeting on their side, politely, privately, and in advance. You can ask if gifts are expected and, if so, what type of gift is expected. Also, try to evaluate your gift from the perspective of the community.

By the way, if you work for government and you don't have money for gifts, don't bring that up. And if your organization doesn't have a budget for gifts, but the community requests a nominal gift such as tobacco, then be prepared to pay for it out of your own pocket; it can be very helpful for the relationship-building process.

If you are offered a gift, by all means accept it, express your appreciation, and consider it a good sign that your relationship building is going well.

QUESTIONS TO EXPECT

Prior to your presentation, you and your team will need to consider the kinds of questions the community will likely ask you: first, within the scope of your proposed business venture or project and its potential impacts on the community; second, beyond the project, including your personal and corporate history and values. Be sure to prepare your responses to those anticipated questions in advance of the first meeting. The best source of information for questions from the community will be from people who have worked with the community recently. I would ask those same people for advice on how to answer the questions; at least, you can find out what does not work.

Present

If you've worked your way through the RESPECT model so far, then the Research, Examine, and Strategy elements are in place. Now it's time to begin thinking about your presentation to the Indigenous community. Is the objective of the first meeting just to get acquainted? Or is it to reach agreement on how to proceed? If you have money for one meeting only, I suggest making this meeting all about "getting to know you," in the hope of continuing electronically in the future. That's better than trying to achieve more than one goal at your one meeting. Let's look at some key presentation issues, including planning your first meeting, protocol including land acknowledgements, cultural mannerisms, and language use.

YOUR FIRST MEETING

What you might expect from the first meeting depends on many factors. For example, are you a senior manager or a member of the rank and file? Do you have a major role and significant responsibility? Has your organization's prior relationship with the Indigenous community and its leaders been good, bad, or indifferent? Did your organization insert you as the point person in an ongoing dispute because your predecessor was not getting along with the community or its leaders?

Try not to arrive too early to your first meeting. If you do, don't sit down beside people you don't know and start conversations about the weather and the kids. The last thing you want to do is make friends with someone who may not have a good relationship with the community.

When I was doing engagement work, I would hang out by the coffee machine or on the smokers' deck and make small talk with community members and maybe gain an insight or two. I don't smoke or vape, but I have found you can get a good conversation going with someone who does.

Another consideration is whether to bring the maps and plans for your project. Indigenous communities will want to get to know who you are as a person before conducting any serious business. You may have these items with you in a carrying case, but I wouldn't be in a rush to throw them on the table.

Be professional but not impersonal during your first meeting. Follow the lead and mood of the people you are meeting with and expect to listen as much as possible. Be prepared to acknowledge any residential school survivor issues should they come up.

As a customary rule of protocol, one community cannot speak for another community. Strive to avoid setting up processes, discussions, or consultations where this can become an issue.

PROTOCOL: LAND ACKNOWLEDGEMENTS

It can be customary among Indigenous Peoples to acknowledge the host peoples and their territory at the outset of any meeting. It follows, then, that if you want to work effectively with Indigenous Peoples, one of the best ways to start out is by showing respect to the people you are working with. This respect can be established at the beginning of a meeting by following proper protocol and acknowledging the host community, its people, and its territory. In this way, you are acknowledging that the nation has had a relationship with the land you're standing on since time immemorial.

A land acknowledgement is a sign of respect and recognition, and you can't go wrong with respect and recognition. You are acknowledging the ties that Indigenous Peoples have to the land—its importance to their culture, ceremonies, and traditions. Respectful acknowledgement of First Nations protocol has long been the norm at meetings and public events in BC and is now becoming increasingly common across the country.

There are two protocol greetings that you can use at the beginning of your meeting, depending on whether you're on treaty territory or traditional territory. To determine which protocol greeting is appropriate, you will need to do some initial research. Sometimes, it's not so easy to determine on whose treaty or traditional territory you'll be meeting on. When in doubt, ask a member of the community or the local Friendship Centre, or a friend or colleague who has done a similar acknowledgement with the community.

Treaty territory is as it sounds—lands that have been defined through negotiations and that usually, but not always, have an accompanying map to show you the boundaries.

Traditional territory is a little more complicated, but it is usually land that is used and occupied by Indigenous Peoples, although it has not been defined by treaty. In some cases, you can find maps of traditional territories, but take care in relying solely on a map, as the information it contains can be subjective.

||||||||||||||||||||||||||||||||||||||||||||||||||||||||||||||||||||||||||||||||||||||||||||||||||||||||||||||||||||||||||||||||||||

Don't assume that a band is necessarily in its own traditional territory. Throughout Canada, the federal government located bands' reserves far from their traditional territories for different reasons.

||||||||||||||||||||||||||||||||||||||||||||||||||||||||||||||||||||||||||||||||||||||||||||||||||||||||||||||||||||||||||||||||||||

Here are some resources to assist you:

- Find the nearest Friendship Centre and ask. The National Association of Friendship Centres (nafc.ca) links 118 Friendship Centres plus seven provincial and territorial associations.

- The Canadian Association of University Teachers (caut.ca) has developed a useful comprehensive Guide to Acknowledging First Peoples & Traditional Territory.

- Native-Land.ca is a good resource; it's a big map so it takes a bit of time to load and carries a disclaimer that more research might be needed.

- Google Maps launched a project in 2017 to add over three thousand Canadian Indigenous reserves and settlement lands to Google Maps and Google Earth platforms.

- The *Indigenous Peoples Atlas of Canada* is a four-volume atlas created from a collaboration between the Royal Canadian Geographical Society and Indigenous organizations in Canada.

Once you have tackled the difficult task of determining the type of lands you will be meeting on, you can choose the appropriate greeting.

Below are two sample acknowledgements for your review, consideration, and adaptation. Keep in mind that these are not the only ways to acknowledge your hosts, and you may learn of alternative greetings that are more appropriate to your setting. One way to do this is to simply ask the meeting organizer for proper protocol.

Treaty Territory Protocol

"I would like to thank the _____ First Nation(s) for agreeing to meet with us today and for welcoming us to your treaty lands."

Traditional Territory Protocol

"I would like to thank the _____ First Nation(s) for taking the time to meet with us today and for inviting us into your traditional territory."

It's quite likely that in your research you will come across a variety of examples of how to make a land acknowledgement. Some will be short and simple, while others will be more expansive. It's up to you which words to choose and how deep you want to go.

‖‖

An informed acknowledgement is authentic, accurate, respectful, and spoken with heartfelt sincerity. It is not a platitude. The exercise of doing the research to find out on whose land a meeting or event is taking place is an opportunity to open hearts and minds to the past and make a commitment to contributing to a better future, which is the essence of reconciliation.

‖‖

There are different tiers of acknowledgements; which one you use depends on the size of the meeting or event.

- The first tier is a simple acknowledgement of the treaty or traditional land and the people whose history is tied to that land.
- In the next tier, the associated Indigenous culture is included in the opening to the meeting or event.
- The ultimate acknowledgement involves incorporating Indigenous people into the design of the opening and event.

If your meeting or event is in British Columbia, you could include recognition that the land is unceded territory. British Columbia is unique in Canada in that most of the province[3] (an area that's about 95 per cent of the land base, or nearly 900,000 square kilometres) is unceded, non-surrendered First Nations territories—it was never subject to a treaty negotiation. So in BC, the protocol might go as follows:

Traditional Unceded Territory Protocol

"I would like to thank the _____ First Nation(s) for taking the time to meet with us today and for inviting us into your traditional unceded territory."

During your research, you may also find that some communities have protocol guidelines on their website, and that some local governments, universities, and colleges have protocol guidelines for you to follow if you are having a meeting or hosting an event within their bounds.

You can do the acknowledgement or invite someone from the community to do it. Make sure you thank the host nation, and don't stray into welcoming delegates or meeting participants during the acknowledgement. That could offend the host nation and embarrass yourself and your team.

||||||||||||||||||||||||||||||||||||||||||||||||||||||||||||||||||||||||||||||||||||||||||||||||||||||||||||||||||||||||||||||||||||||

Protocol 101

1. Be sure to ask the person with whom you are setting up the meeting to help you with the proper greeting and meeting protocol before you arrive.

2. Keep in mind that your spirit and sincerity can matter more than your particular words.

||||||||||||||||||||||||||||||||||||||||||||||||||||||||||||||||||||||||||||||||||||||||||||||||||||||||||||||||||||||||||||||||||||||

INVITING AN ELDER

If you're going to invite an elder to conduct protocol, it is extremely important that they are treated with respect and their needs are seen to before, during, and after the ceremony. Here are some guidelines and suggestions on elder protocol.

Questions to ask the elder:

- Spelling and pronunciation of their name
- How they should be addressed
- Their contact information

If you are on a first-name basis with an elder, should you use it in public? Be cautious; people may not know you are on a first-name basis and may be offended with your use of the first name.

Determining an appropriate honorarium:

- The honorarium respects the value of what the elder is offering.

- Never ask the elder what you should give them.

- The honorarium should be ascertained before the ceremony—keep in mind that you are asking to impose a monetary value on a sacred ceremony, so be respectful in your dealings.

Travel arrangements:

- Be prepared to cover travelling costs (do you need to send a car or taxi to pick them up?).

- Will they be travelling on their own or with someone?

- Find out the name of their travelling companion and whether or not that person requires payment.

Food and beverages:

- Find out in advance if the elder has allergies or dietary requirements, if they are invited to stay for breakfast, lunch, or dinner.

- In some cultures, it is customary for the elder to be served their food—this is definitely a must if the elder has mobility challenges and can't carry a plate of food while using a walking stick or wheelchair.

- Some elders will not participate in events where alcohol is being served; be sure to include this information when extending the invitation.

When contacting an elder, a phone call is often better than a letter. Elders often rely more on the spoken word than the written word. Do not contact them months in advance and then leave it at that—contact them again a few weeks in advance, and then again a few days in advance. Be prepared that they may have to cancel due to community events or health issues. If that occurs, contact the community again and ask for their advice on inviting another elder.

At the expected time of arrival, have someone at the front door of the building to greet the elder and their travelling companion. Do not assume that they will shake hands. As you are introducing yourself, wait to see if they offer their hand. If they do, do not squeeze their hand—apply pressure no greater than they provide; expect it to be a soft handshake and you will be fine. Be sure to let the person who will introduce and thank the elder know about handshaking considerations.

Elders may include smudging as part of the acknowledgement, so ensure the facility is alerted that there will be smoke in the air. At large events consider having a quiet room where the elder can prepare for the smudge or blessing, or rest after travelling or before returning to their home. Have a snack and a drink available upon their arrival, or if it is midday or evening, plan to have a meal available.

During the ceremony, everyone stands, hats removed, heads bowed, hands by their sides or clasped in front. Don't sit down until you are sure the elder has finished speaking. Do not talk, text, or take phone calls during the ceremony. Be in the moment and ask the group or audience to also be in the moment.

When the elder has completed the ceremony, thank them and their companion. Ensure that they are guided to the quiet room and offer the honorarium at that time, not in front of the group. Once they are ready to make their way home, usher them to the front door and ensure their transportation is ready.

PRONUNCIATIONS

When it comes to pronunciations, people often ask me, "Do I get credit for trying?" No, trying is not enough. Be sure to correctly pronounce the name of the community and any community representatives. Work with your community contacts or cultural centre representatives to learn the pronunciations you need.

Check out community websites for clues and be prepared to seek out help. You could contact the band office and ask if you could employ someone there to help you and your team with pronunciation. If someone from the community is willing to teach you, don't try the words a few times and give up. Keep trying until you get it.

You could also call the local Friendship Centre, band, or community office after hours, listen to the recorded voice message several times, and practise until you get the pronunciation correct—that way you can take as long as you need. The nation's website may include a phonetic pronunciation guide, and any videos on the website will likely refer to the nation. Some provinces also produce guides to phonetic pronunciations.

PARTICIPATING IN CULTURAL EVENTS

At some point during your work with an Indigenous community, you will be expected to participate in a cultural event. It could be an opening prayer, a smudge, or some other form of cultural protocol. It can be unnerving to participate in a smudge for the first time. When in doubt about what to do, ask the host or a friend of the community to explain how to participate. If all else fails, follow the lead of the people in front of you. Just take your time and don't worry about making a mistake—it's your first time, and mistakes happen.

Sometimes at community events, you may be invited to try the community's best food. This invitation is an immense honour, but in some communities, the best food may be incredibly rich in flavour and not for every palate. To decline such an offering would be a serious faux pas. The best thing you can do is try it with your poker face on and say, "Mmm, this is some of the best I have ever tasted."

If you have dietary or religious restrictions, it's smart to inform the person who invites you at the time of invitation. You could say, "I am honoured to be invited but I just can't participate in the meal/feast. Is it all right if I still attend?"

EYE CONTACT

Many non-Indigenous people believe that it is important to maintain eye contact during conversation. For many Indigenous Peoples, continuous eye contact may not be expected or even accepted as a courtesy of conversation. We once asked an elder for his thoughts on eye contact.

He said, "We never used to have much eye contact. When we did, it was only at the start of the meeting. After that, it was not considered important to maintain eye contact."

Another elder commented, "If I had not seen you for a long time, maybe four months or more, then I would look you briefly in the eye and that would be it. Then I would go back to looking around because if we were looking at each other in the eye, we could miss supper going by."

For residential school survivors, making eye contact with school or church officials often led to physical punishment.

If you have the opportunity to attend an Indigenous community event, look at people's eyes and where they are gazing—their gaze is usually not on the speaker. This is not a sign of disrespect. Indigenous listeners are usually more interested in following the speaker's words than where they are gazing.

||||||||||||||||||||||||||||||||||||||||||||||||||||||||||||||||||||||||||||||||||||||||||||||||||||||||||||||||||||||||||||||||||||

Do not expect a lot of eye contact and do not enforce a lot of eye contact.

||||||||||||||||||||||||||||||||||||||||||||||||||||||||||||||||||||||||||||||||||||||||||||||||||||||||||||||||||||||||||||||||||||

HANDSHAKES

When it comes to a handshake and Indigenous Peoples, what could possibly go wrong? Offering a hand for a handshake is a fairly common social practice when meeting people. But remember that when you are working with Indigenous Peoples, you are working across cultures with individuals in their own right. Some Indigenous people do not shake hands and are therefore not expecting or comfortable with a handshake. Be prepared that if you offer a hand, you may not have one offered in return. Should this happen, don't read anything into it. Do not interpret it as a sign of disrespect or a sign that they don't like you; it could be a sign that they simply don't shake hands.

So, what do you do if you offer a handshake and none comes back? You may be left hanging! To save yourself from this uncomfortable situation, you can pretend that you had intended to scratch your shoulder instead. Another possibility is that when you offer a handshake, they offer you the left hand instead—there is no shaking or squeezing and it can go on for an uncomfortably long period. Remember, they are just being polite. Your job is to roll with it.

Let others lead the handshake. If they grab your hand firmly and squeeze really hard twice while doing the salt-and-pepper-shaker action, then do that in return. But don't lead, in case they don't do any of it. There have been situations in which Indigenous people have been caught off guard in a handshake situation and have had their hands squeezed too hard and have been injured—not a good way to start off your Indigenous relations.

When working in the north, be sure to remove your glove when shaking hands.

A last word on handshakes: you know you are doing really well when you are given a hug instead of a handshake!

ACRONYMS AND TECHNICAL TERMS

We have attended many meetings in Indigenous communities and have witnessed first-hand how visitors overuse acronyms. Acronyms may make great sense but only to those using them. Remember where you are and who your audience is. Not only will many in your Indigenous audience be unfamiliar with your acronyms, they might not even want to learn them!

Indigenous Peoples are like audiences anywhere in the sense that they want a presentation that they can relate to and understand. One comment we often hear from Indigenous community members is "How come the presenters have to use such big words?"

Make your presentation appeal to your audience. If the audience consists of strictly technical people, then technical terms and jargon will be welcome. Otherwise, use language that a lay person can understand. If in doubt, explain things in plain language that everyone can understand, usually at about a high school level. This approach will help you communicate with a large audience.

COLLOQUIALISMS

When working with Indigenous Peoples, it is wise to avoid the use of colloquialisms. Many colloquial expressions in popular communication carry connotations that may offend at least some of the people you will meet.

Circle the wagons: "Circle the wagons" is akin to saying, "The savages are coming." Not all relationships with Indigenous Peoples required a circling of the wagons.

Indian summer: An "Indian summer" is a late summer; the inference is that Indians are always late. Many people respond, "But I use this phrase in the highest respect as referring to a beautiful time of year." It may not be your intention to offend anyone, but the phrase has a history and, by using it, you may have a negative impact on the people you're working with.

Indian time: The inference of "Indian time" is that Indians are always late. You may hear this term being used by Indigenous Peoples, but don't let that use lull you into thinking it's okay for you to use it. This is an example of stereotyping, and the use of stereotypes among members of the same group (race, culture, nation, sport, gender, sexual orientation) is different from the use of stereotypes between members of different groups, whatever the groups' dynamics.

Low man on the totem pole: Totem poles are very sacred items to the people who carve and display them. Avoid this expression. Did you know that in some Indigenous communities, being low on the totem pole is actually a higher honour than being on the top?

Off the reservation: I have two issues with the expression "off the reservation." The first is that "reservation" is an American term, and if you use it in Canada, they will know you are a rookie and treat you accordingly. In Canada, they are called "reserves" under the *Indian Act*. My second issue with the expression is that it is used to make people sound like they have outrageous requests or even make them sound crazy, as in "Bob, you're off the reservation with that request."

Powwow: "We need to get together and have a powwow to discuss this." A powwow can be a significant community event. This type of everyday reference to it may annoy some members of the community.

Too many chiefs and not enough Indians: A good friend told me a story about a meeting he attended in the course of his consulting work with a large organization. The organization had many people from many different departments working on a relationship-building initiative. During the meeting, it became evident that direction was lacking. Our friend said, "We have a problem. It seems to me that we have too many chiefs and not enough Indians." The ensuing silence went on forever—he said it was perhaps the most embarrassing moment of his life. Fortunately, he had a good relationship in the community and that moment became a long-running joke around the multi-party table. The Indigenous representatives took every opportunity to remind him of the "Indian chief surplus problem." Needless to say, such expressions no longer have a place in his business vocabulary.

TERMS TO AVOID

Here are some commonly used terms I suggest you take pains to avoid. Mind you, these are simply my "suffering is optional" recommendations. But if you do use any of these expressions, you may face an extra hour of meeting time, if not more.

Canada's Indigenous Peoples: The inference of expressions like "Canada's Indigenous Peoples" is that Canada *owns* Indigenous Peoples. In principle 18 of Gregory Younging's excellent *Elements of Indigenous Style: A Guide for Writing By and About Indigenous Peoples*, he writes, "Indigenous Peoples are independent sovereign nations that predate Euro-colonial states and are not 'owned' by Euro-colonial states." Therefore, appropriate usage "avoids the use of possessives that imply this, such as 'Canada's Indigenous Peoples,' 'our Indigenous Peoples,' and 'the Indigenous Peoples of Canada.'"[4]

The appropriate phrasing is "Indigenous Peoples in Canada," or "the Indigenous population in Winnipeg." "Indigenous people of Canada" is at best generalizing and at most meaningless.

Crown land(s): "Crown land" or "Crown lands" is a familiar term that should be used with much more caution than it typically is. How often have you heard outdoors enthusiasts refer to camping on Crown land, for example? The Crown—that is, the federal and provincial governments—doesn't own the land outright, despite what the term suggests. As mentioned earlier, British Columbia is unique in Canada in that most of the province is unceded, which means Aboriginal Title has neither been surrendered nor acquired by the Crown. This distinction can best be seen in the *Delgamuukw and Gisday'way* decision of 1997 in which the Supreme Court of Canada states that Aboriginal Title represents an encumbrance on the Crown's ultimate title in cases where it has not been ceded, released, or surrendered in a treaty.

Equality: Aboriginal Peoples aren't treated equally because they exist under a separate set of laws, the *Indian Act*, and they are recognized in the *Constitution Act*.

The *Indian Act* is actually a study in contradictions. Its purpose was to assimilate, but in practice it segregated and marginalized Aboriginal Peoples; restricted their ability to be part of the local economy; forced children to attend separate schools, often far away from their families; outlawed their traditions, language, and culture; and restricted their ability to mingle with mainstream Euro-settlers.

There is no equality in the standard of living for people living on-reserve. More often than not, those who live on-reserve have to contend with poor housing and unsafe water, both of which contribute to poorer health; lower levels of education, which leads to lower rates of employment; and higher rates of incarceration.

Prior to 1960, Aboriginal Peoples were denied the right to vote. Well, they could vote if they gave up their Indian status and treaty rights, but then they were denied certain rights that came with living under the *Indian Act*.

The *Constitution Act, 1982*, also puts Aboriginal Peoples, the term used in the Act, in a different constitutional category than other Canadians. Section 35 recognizes and affirms existing Aboriginal and Treaty Rights, which is not done for other peoples.

As long as there is the *Indian Act* and the *Constitution Act*, there will never be "equality," as is often called for in rhetorical conversation. When Indigenous Peoples hear the terms "equal" or "equality," they hear that they would have to give up their constitutionally protected rights in order to be afforded that equality. They hear, "We can be equal only if we give up our human rights to be who we are as a people."

So if the subject of equality comes up, such as in the claim "We're all equal here!" see it for what it is—a rhetorical aspiration that would be incredibly hard to achieve without constitutional reform.

"I have a Ph.D. in land use planning": Touting your credentials is problematic. Phrases like "I have a Ph.D. in land use planning" carry a sense of authority, and many Indigenous people, due to experiences in residential schools and from living under the *Indian Act*, have issues with those who present themselves as authority figures. One reaction might be "What can *you* possibly tell us about our lands that we have lived on for thousands of years?" It is much better to take a humbler approach and say, "I have lots to share and lots to learn, and I look forward to working with this community."

Prehistory: Avoid using the term "prehistory"; it implies that the history of Indigenous Peoples began with the arrival of Europeans and the written records of their travels, impressions, and experiences. In reality, each individual Indigenous culture has its own creation story that certainly predates the arrival of Europeans in what is now known as Canada.

A related caution is to avoid saying that the Americas were "discovered." When Christopher Columbus arrived in the Americas, an estimated 100 million Indigenous Peoples[5] were living there.

A better way to divide the timeline is "pre-contact" and "post-contact."

Special rights: On the flip side of the equality coin are Aboriginal Rights, which some people choose to describe as "special rights" or race-based rights, particularly in respect to hunting and fishing rights.

The rights of Aboriginal Peoples were originally established in the Royal Proclamation of 1763. The Royal

Proclamation recognized Aboriginal Rights to harvest resources from Aboriginal Peoples' traditional territories, declared "as their Hunting Grounds." But it wasn't until more than two hundred years later, in 1996, that Aboriginal Rights were recognized in the Supreme Court of Canada and confirmed in *R. v. Van der Peet*; this case established a test by which to prove Aboriginal Rights. Chief Justice Antonio Lamer wrote:

> The doctrine of aboriginal rights exists... because of one simple fact: when Europeans arrived in North America, Aboriginal peoples *were already here*, living in communities on the land, and participating in distinctive cultures, as they had done for centuries. It is this fact, and this fact above all others, which separates aboriginal peoples from all other minority groups in Canadian society and which mandates their special legal... status.[6]

Aboriginal Rights should never be referred to as special rights. There is no alternative phrase for Aboriginal Rights.

Indigenous Peoples differentiate themselves from others in the body politic in that they did not come here from anywhere. For example, if you are Gwawaenuk in the Broughton Archipelago, as I am, then you are from nowhere else in the world. Contrast this with people from other cultures who have come to Canada at some period in history, and you can see the distinction. In this sense, Aboriginal Rights—or Section 35 rights, as they are sometimes called by Indigenous Peoples—are human rights.

Stakeholders: "Stakeholder" is a blanket term used to describe an individual, group, or organization that stands to be affected by the outcome of a project. The problem with blanket terms is that they tend to be used indiscriminately, so there's a potential to offend.

Aboriginal Title was first recognized by King George III in the Royal Proclamation of 1763, yet Aboriginal Peoples continue to struggle to have their constitutionally protected rights recognized. They are "Rights and Title holders," not "stakeholders," so avoid this term at all costs.

If non-Aboriginal stakeholders take issue with a project, they have the freedom and the right to lobby the government to try to effect change. They can also engage in negative media campaigns and hold protests. If an Aboriginal community has issues with a project, they can do the same. But, and this is the crux of the difference, because they have constitutionally protected rights, Aboriginal Peoples also have the ability to tie up a project in a legal process. Aboriginal communities are not mere stakeholders, they are *Rights holders*. And that's the term that should be used.

"We're here to help": "The most terrifying words in the English language are 'I'm from the government and I'm here to help,'" said Ronald Reagan. "We're here to help" was also an all-too-familiar refrain used by Indian agents of the past, on behalf of the federal government, to describe laws and policies of the *Indian Act* designed to "help" Aboriginal Peoples become something other than who they were. The prime minister at the time the Act was passed, John A. Macdonald, referred to Indigenous Peoples as "savages," and all policies were ostensibly for the betterment of the savages, to "raise them up" and assimilate them into mainstream Euro-Canadian settler society. As Macdonald said to the House of Parliament:

> When the school is on the reserve, the child lives with its parents, who are savages, and though he may learn to read and write, his habits and training mode of thought are Indian. He is simply a savage who can read and write.[7]

All those offers to "help" were not generated by a desire to be of service—they were generated by a federal policy that was designed for cultural assimilation and was so severe in nature that, as noted earlier, former chief justice of Canada Beverley McLachlin described it as cultural genocide.

With that in mind, you can see that while you may have the purest of intentions, it's best to avoid saying you're here to help altogether. It's better to put the situation in the light of learning from each other and engaging in joint problem-solving. You could say, "I have a lot to share, but I know that I also have a lot to learn."

"Your file": Don't refer to a community as a "file," as in "I'm here to talk to you because I was just given your file." The community may interpret this phrase as meaning all they are is a file, instead of actually people or a community. The phrase instantly calls to mind the *Indian Act*, with the community as one more file—"like all the others"—in that legal document.

Instead, talk to the community about the work that has been done and about how you're looking forward to working together to solve problems or find solutions.

||||||||||||||||||||||||||||||||||||||||||||||||||||||||||||||||||||||||||||||||||||||||||||||||||||||||||||||||

It can be very hard to achieve blanket solutions or approaches, so try not to expect them to work. Adapt your approach to the particular people and place.

||||||||||||||||||||||||||||||||||||||||||||||||||||||||||||||||||||||||||||||||||||||||||||||||||||||||||||||||

HONOUR YOUR WORD

Most of the pre-contact Indigenous Peoples of the Americas lived in oral societies. Very few of them had written languages or histories, but that is not to say that they didn't record their histories in other ways. One of the most important ways was through the oral tradition of storytelling. The Supreme Court of Canada has declared that oral histories must be given the same legal weight as written histories in Aboriginal Rights and Title cases.

In Indigenous culture, your word is more important than anything written on a piece of paper. Some communities have had problems with people not honouring their word, so your meetings might be recorded.

At all costs, you must make sure that you protect your word and integrity in all your dealings on behalf of your organization. Nothing can damage your reputation more than having to say, "Things have changed, and I will no longer be able to deliver what I promised."

Because the traditional mode of Indigenous communication is oral, speech nuances like tone, tempo, volume, and inflections can be very important. Be aware of the community style of speech and match it if you can, without trying to copy their accent. And don't be in a rush to respond until you figure out the tempo of the conversation.

⸻

In an oral society, the spoken word can be more important than any written contract. Guard your word from changes in organizational direction. Don't offer things that you're not certain you can deliver, and definitely follow up on the things you said you would do.

⸻

HAVE THEY REALLY FINISHED SPEAKING?

A chief was making introductory comments to a meeting of company and government employees. The talk went on for a few minutes, and then the chief paused to gather more thoughts. The lead person for the company thought that the chief had finished and began to respond to his comments. The company spokesman completed a sentence or two before the chief interrupted him by saying, "I'm not finished yet."

⸻

Non-Indigenous conversations often follow a brisk pattern of "point-counterpoint." When working with Indigenous Peoples, be sure to leave time for the speaker to finish, especially in a new relationship.

⸻

SENSE OF HUMOUR

Do you have a good sense of humour? Can you laugh at yourself? Can you take it when people are laughing at you? We have seen many visitors welcomed to Indigenous community meetings with humour that sometimes bites a little. Go with the flow. Being teased with humour can be a sign of acceptance—signaling that community members may want to work with you and are trying to get you to conform to group norms.

WHERE ARE YOU FROM?

One of the better questions to ask when getting to know an Indigenous person is "Where are you from?" It's more a question of "Who are your people and where is your territory?" This is different from "Where do you live?" If the person replies, "I'm living in Vancouver," you may have uncovered an important clue about the role that person plays in the community. It could be that this person has left the community temporarily for education or management training and is being groomed as a future leader. Or it could be that they were adopted out and do not have intimate community knowledge or involvement.

If the reply describes a place in the community's traditional territory, then you might guess that the person is more connected to the community and therefore is more knowledgeable and concerned regarding its interests. But more questions are probably needed before you can properly assess this person's place in, and perspective on, the community. Obviously, you can't ask, "Where you are from?" when meeting in the band office, but you could say, "What a beautiful community. Did you grow up here?" They may not have, which means you just discovered an important piece of information.

THE CONCEPT OF FAMILY

Within Indigenous communities, "family" means different things to different people. You might be tempted to assume that family means immediate family, including husband or wife, children, and perhaps grandparents. For some Indigenous communities, the concept can have broader meaning. For example, first cousins can be considered as close as brothers and sisters. This can mean a larger role for families and more family members in community activities. In a few cases, I have seen the concept of family applied to the whole community—meaning that the whole community, all 377 people, are a family grouping.

COMMUNAL THINKING

Read recent court decisions on Aboriginal Rights and Title and you will find that they reference communally held rights. Generally speaking, Aboriginal Rights are collectively held on behalf of the entire community. Therefore, any decision regarding the use of those lands is a potential infringement on the rights of the whole community. Indigenous communities plan to be in the area forever. They feel no pressure to make short-term decisions on matters that can affect the long-term interests of the community and its future generations. The larger the decision, the more the community will be involved.

It is also important to note that land use decisions are usually not made under leadership discretion or by majority rule but rather by broad community support. What can you do to avoid getting into trouble? Allow more time in your project timeline to accommodate a broader community decision-making process and accede to a chief's request for more time for additional community discussions. See "Your Timeline Is Your Problem" under Strategize, earlier in this chapter.

Evaluate

Any meeting with an Indigenous community, or one of its members, should be followed by an evaluation of how things have gone so far. The process of considering what worked and what didn't work is fairly simple.

Ask yourself:

- How did the meeting go?
- What questions did community members ask?
- What questions remain outstanding?
- What concerns did the community raise about your proposed project?
- How satisfied were they with your answers?
- What community concerns about the project remain outstanding?
- How critical are those concerns to the viability of the project?
- What was the tone of the meeting?
- What was the apparent perspective of the chief and council members?
- What was the apparent perspective of community elders?
- Who holds effective political power in the community?
- What do those power brokers think about your project?

Customize

You'll have completed a great deal of work to reach this level of Working Effectively with Indigenous Peoples®. Now is the time to customize your work, incorporating the feedback received and requests made during your journey through the RESPECT model.

When designing your work process or plan, consider customizing the following areas according to the needs and priorities of the Indigenous community with which you are working:

- Legal capacity
- Human resources capacity
- Communications capacity
- Financial capacity
- Timelines
- Workforce development capacity
- Business development capacity

INDIGENOUS COMMUNITY COMMUNICATIONS

Of particular importance in the Customize step is community communication. Indigenous communities communicate internally in various ways. Like all communities, sometimes there is efficient communication and other times there is not. Because Aboriginal Rights are collectively held, it's important to know if the community is aware of what is going on. Here are some things you should know about the process of Indigenous community communication.

- As we've discussed, Indigenous Peoples are traditionally oral societies. Within the framework of an oral society, word can travel remarkably quickly from one person to the next. This can occur in community events, on the telephone, through social media, or in casual conversation. The combination of better telecommunications infrastructure in many remote communities, combined with the rise of social media, has also had an impact on community communications.

- Facebook, at this point, seems to the leading platform adopted in communities because it's a conduit for communication between community members regardless of where they are located. As more people leave communities for education and employment opportunities in urban centres, Facebook is a means of staying in touch. Another aspect of Facebook usage is its value in emergency alerts for remote communities and as a means of locating family members following an evacuation due to fire or flood. As new social media platforms emerge, Facebook may be superseded by other platforms.

- Community communications may not be structured the way that a corporate person would expect. If you were to call the band office and ask to speak to the communications manager, chances are you would find there is no such person. Many communities do not have a formal structured communications process with a vice president or director of communications. Work will have to be done to figure out the informal communications process and structure. Ask yourself:
  - Do chief, council, and band administration communicate regularly and well with the community?

- Is community communication fast or slow? (If there is no formal structure, then assume that communication is slow until you determine otherwise.)

- Lack of communication, poor communication, or slow communication could be an issue. Be prepared to suggest or offer help to ensure that key issues are being communicated.

- Overcrowded housing is an issue on reserves Canada-wide. Single-family dwellings will sometimes house multiple families. Direct-mail campaigns can be problematic if this issue is not considered, as not all residents of a dwelling will have access to the mail.

For big decisions, the more the community knows, and the wider that community knowledge is shared, the better the decision and the stronger the support. You need to know if the full community is receiving your information or message. If not, then you must find a way to reach them all. Consider the following methods as a starting point:

- Organize presentations in town hall format
- Advertise in community and regional newspapers
- Conduct a direct-mail campaign to individual community members
- Make presentations on community radio or television
- Distribute joint newsletters with the community
- If permitted, post information on community bulletin boards at the band office, recreation centre, health centre, and so on

- Post information about meetings on social media platforms

||||||||||||||||||||||||||||||||||||||||||||||||||||||||||||||||||||||||||||||||||||||||||||||||||||||||||||||||||||

Two key points:

1. You must ensure that the whole community knows what is happening from your organization's perspective.

2. You must ensure that you are receiving widespread feedback from the community.

||||||||||||||||||||||||||||||||||||||||||||||||||||||||||||||||||||||||||||||||||||||||||||||||||||||||||||||||||||

When you have concluded the Customize step, the next move is to go back to the community with another presentation—thereby demonstrating your commitment to adapt your plans to accommodate the community's key needs and concerns—and seek the community's further feedback.

Transform

If you and your organization have truly followed this RESPECT process, you are now ready to transform your Indigenous community relationships. Return to the community to present your customized presentation. The ideal presentation should include a synopsis of the initial presentation, identification of issues and concerns, and steps that have been taken or that are in progress to address issues and concerns.

Transformation is an ongoing process. It will take continued commitment to transform an arm's-length (and possibly adversarial) relationship to a mutually beneficial long-term relationship, but I know it can be done. On a personal level, strive to maintain the community relationships that you have developed by working through the RESPECT process—for the long-term.

To support the transformation process:

- Continue to participate in community cultural events
- Send information on project employment and procurement opportunities, as well as on related training and scholarship opportunities
- Send information on corporate donations or other programs that may be of interest to the community
- Continue to stay up-to-date on the community and its issues through media alerts
- Visit the community just to stay in touch, when you don't need or want anything

Again, your intention must be to sustain long-term and mutually beneficial relationships between your organization and the Indigenous community. Nothing can hurt you like calling only when you need something. We believe that you can do more on an informal basis than in numerous formal meetings.

||||||||||||||||||||||||||||||||||||||||||||||||||||||||||||||||||||||||||||||||||||||||||||||||||||||||||||||||||||||

At all times, remember that you and your organization are in many cases doing business with a culture, not with another business.

||||||||||||||||||||||||||||||||||||||||||||||||||||||||||||||||||||||||||||||||||||||||||||||||||||||||||||||||||||||

FOLLOWING ALL the steps of the RESPECT model will help you develop and increase your understanding of working with the community. People sometimes say, "We don't have the time to do all this work." I disagree. If you don't do it, you will make many simple mistakes and it will take longer to accomplish what you are trying to achieve. Two hours now can save you two months later.

In Summary...

Do:

- Research the community and governing parties before going to the community.

- Plan activities by taking into account the timing of issues, such as fishing, berry picking, or a death in a community, and take appropriate actions.

- Thank the community for the invitation into their traditional or treaty territory. For example, "I would like to thank the _____ First Nation(s) for agreeing to meet with us and inviting us into your traditional (or treaty) territory."

- Use caution when shaking hands. The typical North American "grab and double pump" may not be needed or appreciated.

- Try to establish a relationship and meet before you need something.

- Recognize that there are many dynamics at play when working with Indigenous Peoples and organizations; try to learn about those dynamics in advance.

- Try to match your team's gender composition with the community's decision-making structure.

- Recognize that individual communities value their autonomy (one Indigenous community cannot speak for another); avoid setting up processes, discussions, or consultations where this could be an issue.

- Do everything you can to avoid sacred land issues by asking good questions and gaining understanding.

- Learn about and stay up-to-date on Indigenous issues and perspectives.

- Understand that internal community communications happen in many different ways and can impact your organization's ability to work effectively with those communities.

- Consider dressing casually for work in the community. In many cases, band offices have more casual dress policies than does corporate Canada.

- Be prepared to have your meetings recorded via audio or video, as some communities have had problems in their dealings with people who were less than honourable in remembering what they said.

- Honour all your agreements, especially your oral agreements. Traditionally, Indigenous communities are oral societies and oral agreements are even more important than written agreements.

- Approach issues with a joint problem-solving attitude.

- Know the difference between a band chief and a hereditary chief before you visit an Indigenous community.

- Be prepared to possibly meet both band chiefs and hereditary chiefs on the same day and in the same meeting.

- Be aware of who you are perceived to be aligned with when working in the community and manage those "people alignment" dynamics.

- Be aware that Aboriginal Rights are communally held and that the whole community may need to be involved in the decision-making process.

- Be aware that cultural survival is a fundamental driver of an Indigenous community's decision-making process.

- Expect to participate in cultural events and ask for protocol guidance from the host.

- Ask people where they are from to learn about where they likely stand on community issues.

- Seek strategic placement for your organization's issues on community meeting agendas.

- Ask the Indigenous community how they want to be consulted. What are their expectations?
- Be prepared to say that you are having a problem and that you are seeking their thoughts on how to solve it.
- Anticipate questions the community may have of your organization and prepare answers to those questions.
- Consider taking Indigenous Corporate Training's Indigenous Awareness and Indigenous Relations courses before you start.

Don't:

- Use acronyms or colloquialisms in your communications with Indigenous Peoples.
- Tell the community you are there to speak to its members as stakeholders.
- Tell them that you have a timeline and that they have to meet it; instead, ask which dates would work best for their community.
- Tell them that you have to treat them equally with others, or that we should all be equal.
- Go to them with a completed draft plan for your project before consultation has started.
- Expect to consult with the same community in the same way on different issues.
- Expect to consult with different communities in the same way on similar issues.
- Assume a nation is necessarily in its own territory.
- Assume that the nation's chief and council are able to make land use decisions regarding other peoples' territories.

- Confuse terms relevant to the community such as mixing up "potluck" with "potlatch" or using "reservation" instead of "reserve."

- Refer to the community members as "Indians" or "Natives"; instead use Indigenous Peoples, First Nations, Métis Peoples, Inuit, or name the specific nation you are visiting.

- Say that some of your best friends are Indigenous Peoples, Indian, First Nations, Métis Peoples, or Inuit.

- Ask them if they know well-known First Nations personalities—for example, Adam Beach, Eden Robinson, or Tanya Tagaq.

- Tell them that you prefer a municipal style of government to a traditional government.

- Ask them if they are going to be Canadian when this is all over.

- Impose or expect direct eye contact.

- Feel that you must answer or fill the silent periods during discussions. These silent periods can be longer than you are accustomed to and may be needed for thought formulation. Try to ensure that the speaker has finished before you contribute to the conversation.

{ 9 }

The Personal Side of Reconciliation

‖‖

U P TO THIS point, we've been talking about how to incorporate reconciliation into your business dealings. But, of course, reconciliation can't be something we think of just from nine to five. We all have roles and responsibilities to contribute to moving this country along the reconciliation continuum, and that includes in our personal relationships. When we prioritize treating each other with respect and recognition, we all stand to gain.

Reconciliation is not solely about policy changes and big fixes. It's also about simple gestures and small measures that add up to lasting impact. So, what can individuals do?

News and Media

Stay up-to-date on Indigenous-related news on CBC Indigenous and APTN. And follow Indigenous-related news on media platforms outside the mainstream—there's much more going on than is featured in mainstream media. Actively listen and read: you may pick up on aspects of an article that you otherwise would have skimmed over or not fully understood.

Discuss the full spectrum of Indigenous-related news with your family and friends, including articles about the arts, language preservation, and more. By including topics that are "good news," you are helping to change the social dynamic that only thinks about Indigenous Peoples in terms of problems.

Reconciliation and MMIWG

Prior to European contact and the ensuing fundamental disruption to the traditional lifestyle of Indigenous communities, women were central to the family, were revered in communities that identified as matriarchal societies, had roles within community government and spiritual ceremonies, and were generally respected for the sacred gifts bestowed upon them by the Creator.

The *Indian Act* has disrespected, ignored, and undermined the role of women in many ways and subjected generations of Indigenous women and their children to a legacy of discrimination. This dissolution of women's stature coupled with the abuses of the residential school system have been linked as significant contributors to the vulnerability of Indigenous women.

That vulnerability is considered the root cause of the extremely high number of Indigenous women who are missing or have been murdered. In October 2004, Amnesty International released the *Stolen Sisters* report, which highlighted a 1996 Canadian government statistic that

Aboriginal women between the ages of twenty-five and forty-four with status under the *Indian Act* are five times more likely than all other women of the same age to die as the result of violence.

A 2014 study by the Royal Canadian Mounted Police estimated the number of missing and murdered Indigenous women from 1980 to 2012 at nearly 1,200. Prior to this report, no attempt had been made at the national level to identify how many Indigenous women and girls have been murdered or have gone missing. Indigenous women were invisible in life and invisible in death.

In 2016, the Government of Canada launched an independent National Inquiry into Missing and Murdered Indigenous Women and Girls (MMIWG). The inquiry wrapped up in December 2018, and its final report is due by April 2019.

The vulnerability of Indigenous women in Canada and the violence against them drew the attention of the United Nations. The UN special rapporteur on violence against women, Dubravka Šimonović, visited Canada in 2018 and included the following in her report:

> Indigenous women from First Nations, Metis and Inuit communities are overtly disadvantaged within their societies and in the larger national scheme. Indigenous women face marginalization, exclusion and poverty because of institutional, systemic, multiple, intersecting forms of discrimination that has not been addressed adequately by the State.
>
> Indigenous women have been discriminated historically even by the law; the *Indian Act* provided that First Nations women should not be given the same choice of

status if they married men outside their communities and although this law prevailed for more than a century, reforms still fall short in providing equality to indigenous women and their descendants, which further results in the unequal access of benefits and services.[1]

In order for the status quo to change, there must be a fundamental improvement in education, employment, housing, and health of all Indigenous Peoples. Additionally, the existing discriminatory legislation, including gender discrimination under the *Indian Act*, must be reformed. But we as individual Canadians can contribute significantly to changing the status quo.

~~~~~~

Tips for Reconciliation on a Personal Level

Here are some suggestions for reconciliation regarding MMIWG:

- Attend a Sisters in Spirit vigil every October 4.
- Attend a Strawberry Ceremony every February 14.
- Support the Native Women's Association of Canada.
- Write to your local member of Parliament and ask them to support the introduction of specific criminal provisions related to forced sterilization of some Indigenous women.
- Support a local women's shelter.
- Do not perpetuate the sexualization of Indigenous women by dressing up or dressing your daughters up as "Poco-hotties."

- Watch *Survival, Strength, Sisterhood: Power of Women in the Downtown Eastside,* a short film by Alejandro Zuluaga and Harsha Walia available on Vimeo.

- Read *Our Women and Girls Are Sacred: Interim Report; The National Inquiry into Missing and Murdered Indigenous Women and Girls* (available at mmiwg-ffada.ca).

- Read *Restoring the Balance: First Nations Women, Community, and Culture,* edited by Gail Guthrie Valaskakis, Madeline Dion Stout, and Eric Guimond (University of Manitoba Press, 2009).

∿∿∿∿∿∿∿∿∿∿∿∿∿∿∿∿∿∿∿∿∿∿∿∿∿∿∿∿∿

Reconciliation and Cultural Appropriation

Cultural appropriation is generally defined as the adoption or theft of icons, rituals, aesthetic standards, and behaviour from one culture or subculture by another. Indigenous culture has long been a popular target for appropriation on fashion shoots, for team mascots, and annually at Halloween. "Borrowing" from another culture is symptomatic of the history of colonialism in which the colonizing culture assumes everything from the colonized culture is there for the taking. It is culturally disrespectful to randomly pluck popularized images of a marginalized culture for entertainment without respect for or understanding of the culture.

Cultural appropriation contributes to the endangerment of Indigenous women. The example of the "sexy Native" costume that appears every Halloween perpetuates harmful and dangerous stereotypes that contribute to sexual violence against and human trafficking of Indigenous women and girls. When a woman of non-Indigenous heritage dresses up as the "sexy Native," she demeans Indigenous women and insults the hundreds of missing and murdered Indigenous women and all those who love them. She is unwittingly contributing to the endangerment of Indigenous women and girls.

Another display of cultural appropriation is the naming of sports teams and mimicry of Indigenous Peoples in the design of team mascots and logos. Supporters of this form of appropriation sometimes claim that the use of Indigenous-themed names, logos, and mascots is intended to honour Indigenous groups and educate their fans. In reality, this use reduces Indigenous Peoples to cartoon figures (dehumanizing them) and demeans and diminishes Indigenous self-esteem and cultural pride. It can also lead to team supporters dressing up in culturally disrespectful costumes.

When we understand what cultural appropriation is, why it's harmful, disrespectful, and can even contribute to endangering Indigenous women and girls, then as a country, we are reconciling.

We hope that all Canadians will want to learn about Indigenous Peoples, their cultures, their pre-contact lives, and the impacts of colonization. It is through education that people will understand that Indigenous Peoples have struggled tremendously for a very long time to protect and preserve their culture, how they were forced to change the way they lived, spoke, celebrated, and worshipped. Cultural appropriation demeans that struggle.

~~~~~~

Tips for Reconciliation on a Personal Level

Here are some ways to practise cultural appreciation instead of cultural appropriation:

- If you admire an aspect of another culture, then learn about it and purchase items directly from a person of that culture. If you like the look of Cowichan sweaters, don't buy a "Cowichan-inspired" sweater from a retail giant, buy from a Coast Salish knitter or an Indigenous-owned store that buys sweaters from the knitters. That is cultural respect.

- Don't refer to a culture or a people as exotic. That emphasizes their "otherness." Their culture is not exotic to them; it's who they are and what is important to them.

- Don't assume that it's okay to "borrow" aspects from another culture. In many Indigenous cultures, strict and ancient protocols dictate who can sing certain songs, perform certain dances, and tell certain stories. We don't just take from one another.

~~~~~~

Reconciliation and the Responsibility to Purchase Authentic Indigenous Art

Indigenous art has been coveted ever since European contact with Indigenous Peoples. Explorers were instructed to collect "exotic curiosities," such as ceremonial regalia, clothing, and tools. That desire to possess a piece of "wild" or "exotic" art, unfortunately, led to the manipulation of situations or outright pillaging of communities, sometimes when they were at their most vulnerable and struggling with epidemics, famine, or poverty. Some villages that were empty because of disease or forced relocation were looted. The *Indian Act* made potlatches illegal (from 1880 to 1951), but some potlatch families defied the law and were subjected to raids, imprisonment, and confiscation of masks and regalia, which were often sold to collectors or sold and then donated to museums.

Today, the copying or theft of Indigenous art is less dramatic but more pervasive. Across the country, sales of knock-off items created in Canada and offshore are rampant. Art is the conduit that keeps a culture strong: it connects the present with the past and is an important aspect of identity. It is also an important source of income for communities where economic opportunities can be limited. As the older Indigenous generation ages and passes on, and as economic pressures force more Indigenous Peoples to relocate to urban centres, there is a great responsibility for communities to ensure their culture and art is protected and kept alive by the younger generations.

〰〰〰〰〰〰〰〰〰〰〰〰〰〰〰〰〰〰〰〰〰

Tips for Reconciliation on a Personal Level

What can you do to ensure you are buying authentic Indigenous art?

- If you are buying from a gallery, talk to the owner/staff about the piece you are interested in. Ask about the artist, their community, their other work. If answers to your questions are vague, that could be a sign that the item is not art but a knock-off.

- Many artists have websites, so you can contact them directly.

- If you are a traveller, support authentic Indigenous artists in the country you are visiting.

- If you are a store owner, please don't support the trade of knock-off Indigenous art.

ᗊᗊᗊᗊᗊᗊᗊᗊᗊᗊᗊᗊᗊᗊᗊᗊᗊᗊᗊᗊᗊᗊᗊᗊ

Reconciliation and Reading

Reading this book and others like it will create a foundation for understanding the relationship: what happened, why it happened, and how we can prevent it from happening again. We've included a list of additional resources, including books, films, and websites, as appendix IV to help you as you continue your education.

There is an irony in talking about books written by a culture known for its oral traditions. Indigenous Peoples are the ultimate storytellers, and that inherent skill is finding new and vital expression. It's such an exciting time for all Canadians as these voices emerge and take centre stage for literary awards, on bestseller lists, in bookstores, and in public and home libraries.

There's been an explosion of Indigenous authors and it's really great to see how the reading public has responded. Just two years ago, it would have been unlikely that a book about the *Indian Act* could be a national bestseller or that there would be a book called *Elements of Indigenous Style*.

〰〰〰〰〰〰〰〰〰〰〰〰〰〰〰〰〰〰〰〰〰

Tips for Reconciliation on a Personal Level

Here are some ways in which you can support Indigenous authors:

- Recommend books by Indigenous authors to your book club.
- Buy, read, and gift a wide variety of non-fiction and fiction books by Indigenous authors.
- Read books by Indigenous authors to the children in your life.
- Attend a reading by an Indigenous author.

〰〰〰〰〰〰〰〰〰〰〰〰〰〰〰〰〰〰〰〰〰

Reconciliation and Children

It's the next generation that is really going to carry change forward in Canada. If you have children in your life, the most important thing you can do for reconciliation is to raise informed, compassionate citizens.

Talk to them about residential schools. It's a hard topic, but there are books on the topic for readers of all ages. The history of residential schools is likely now being taught in some manner in your child's school. Support the teachers by talking to your children about the schools and how the schools' impact continues to affect people their own age. Discuss how the *Indian Act* and residential schools are the root causes of many of the issues and challenges Indigenous Peoples live with daily.

Thousands of schools now support Orange Shirt Day (September 30). This movement, which is sweeping the country, officially began in 2013. But it actually began in 1973 when six-year-old Phyllis Webstad entered St. Joseph's Mission Residential School, outside of Williams Lake, BC. Young Phyllis was wearing a brand-new orange shirt for her first day of school—new clothes being a rare and wonderful thing for a First Nations girl growing up in her grandmother's care—but the Missionary Oblates quickly stripped her of her new shirt and replaced it with the school's uniform. While she only attended for one year, the impact was felt in Ms. Webstad's life for many years: "That feeling of worthlessness and insignificance, ingrained in me from my first day at the mission, affected the way I lived my life for many years. Even now, when I know nothing could be further than the truth, I still sometimes feel that I don't matter."[2]

Ms. Webstad's story is the nucleus for what has become a national movement to recognize the experience of survivors of Indian Residential Schools, honour them, and show a collective commitment to ensure that every child matters. The initiative calls for every Canadian to wear an orange shirt on September 30 in the spirit of healing and reconciliation. The date was chosen because that was the time of the year the trucks and buses would enter the communities to "collect" the children and deliver them to their harsh new reality of cultural assimilation; mental, sexual, and physical abuse; shame; and deprivation.

It's extremely heartening to see how this initiative has captivated people. Next September 30, look around and you are bound to see orange T-shirts on people of all ages. If you want to organize an Orange Shirt Day in your workplace, plan ahead! Stores that supply T-shirts sometimes sell out in all sizes long before September 30. Contact your child's school, or a school near you, to find out where the T-shirts are available, as well as the name and community of the Indigenous artist who contributed that year's design. Take a photo of your team in your T-shirts, post it on your website, and share it on social media. Make sure you include the slogan "Every Child Matters" on your shirts.

∧∧∧∧∧∧∧∧∧∧∧∧∧∧∧∧∧∧∧∧∧∧∧∧∧∧∧∧∧∧∧∧∧∧∧∧∧∧

Tips for Reconciliation on a Personal Level

Here are some tips for working with children on reconciliation:

- Talk to children about stereotypes and how to recognize stereotypical references.

- Explain why Indigenous imagery is wrong, for example, in mascots.

- Plan to attend a cultural event, such as a powwow, that is open to the public.

- Learn with them in advance about the powwow culture, the regalia, and the history of the dances.

- Join communities as they celebrate National Indigenous Peoples Day every year on June 21.

∧∧∧∧∧∧∧∧∧∧∧∧∧∧∧∧∧∧∧∧∧∧∧∧∧∧∧∧∧∧∧∧∧∧∧∧∧∧

Conclusion

IIIIIIIIIIIIIIIIIIIIIIIIIIIIIIIIIIIIIIIIIIIIIIII

Reconciliation is about establishing and maintaining a mutually respectful relationship between Aboriginal and non-Aboriginal peoples in this country. In order for that to happen, there has to be awareness of the past, acknowledgement of the harm that has been inflicted, atonement for the causes, and action to change behaviour.

Truth and Reconciliation Commission of Canada[1]

W E ARE AT a very exciting juncture. Everywhere there are signs of constructive long-term change. Cities are renaming streets with Indigenous names and the names of parks are being returned to their original Indigenous names. A surge of people, institutions, corporations, and governments are keen to learn the history that was denied us all in school and to work on reconciliation strategies. I know this because demand for our training has exploded in the past few years.

Granted, there will always be frustrating delays in adjusting public opinion and shifting government policy. It takes time to move a mountain! But if we all individually commit to reconciliation and use the tips, hints, and suggestions provided in this book, we will collectively create a better Canada.

||||||||||||||||||||||||||||||||||||||||||||||||||||||||||||||||||||||||||||||||||||||||||||||||||||||||||||||||||||||||||||||||||||||||||||||||||||

I want you to dream and imagine with me what reconciliation could look like in twenty, thirty, forty years from now. When we are reconciled we will live together in harmony, be gentle with one another, we will be caring and compassionate. When we are reconciled, every person living here will live with dignity, purpose, and value.

CHIEF DR. ROBERT JOSEPH, O.B.C., O.C., RECONCILIATION CANADA AMBASSADOR[2]

||||||||||||||||||||||||||||||||||||||||||||||||||||||||||||||||||||||||||||||||||||||||||||||||||||||||||||||||||||||||||||||||||||||||||||||||||||

Reconciliation is about staying the course. If you take Confederation in 1867 as the formal starting point of the breakdown of the settlers' relationship with Indigenous Peoples, then it's apparent that a relationship that has been dysfunctional for more than 150 years is not going to become functional overnight or even over decades. It's going to take a long time to fix. There are going to be setbacks, but we cannot allow setbacks and disappointments to deter us from the goal of reconciliation.

Acknowledgements

|||||||||||||||||||||||||||||||||||||||||||||||||||||||||||||||||||||||||||||||||||||||||||||||||||

THIS BOOK WOULD not have happened without you. Thank you for your interest in learning how to have respectful and successful relationships with Indigenous Peoples and communities. The intensity of interest in reconciliation on the part of so many Canadians is inspiring.

This book wouldn't have happened without the knowledge, research, and support of my way better half, Cindy Joseph. Together we have built an Indigenous relations training business and provided numerous resources and books to assist Canadians on their journey of reconciliation. We're grateful to all those who have taken our courses. We wanted to broaden the scope of the content for our core course, *Working Effectively with Indigenous Peoples®*, so that it is of value to a wider audience; it was the starting place for *Indigenous Relations*.

To my family and friends who have shared their wisdom and insight with me over the years, thank you.

This is our second collaboration with the remarkable teams at Page Two, Raincoast Books, and ZG Communications, and both experiences have been exemplary.

Finally, I would like to acknowledge Julie for her long and tireless effort toward editing the book and her dedication to the blog. It is her remarkable drive to educate people about creating better Indigenous relations that contributes to the success of everything she does. Thank you.

Pledges of Reconciliation

IIIIIIIIIIIIIIIIIIIIIIIIIIIIIIIIIIIIIIIIIIIIIIIIIIIIIIIIIIIIIIIIIIIIIIIIIIIIIIIIIIIIIIIIIIIIIIIIIIIIIIIIIIIIII

NOW THAT YOU'VE come this far along your path toward reconciliation, here are two Pledges of Reconciliation, one personal and one professional, that you can photo-copy and pin up on your office wall or fridge.

Personal Pledge of Reconciliation with Indigenous Peoples

||||||||||||||||||||||||||||||||||||||||||||||||||||||||||||||||||||||||||||||||||||||||||||||||||||||||||||||||||||

In the spirit of reconciliation with Indigenous Peoples in Canada,

I, _____ , solemnly pledge to:

1 Learn more about Indigenous Peoples and issues.

2 Continue to look forward to positive change for the situation of Indigenous Peoples.

3 Find ways to address the Indigenous-related myths and misconceptions with my fellow Canadians.

4 Not perpetuate stereotypes in my conversations or observations.

5 Encourage others around me to keep reconciliation an ongoing effort.

6 Read the Truth and Reconciliation Commission of Canada's 94 Calls to Action.

7 Actively encourage ongoing support of National Indigenous Peoples Day every June 21 for myself, my family, and my community.

_____ Signature _____ Date

Professional Pledge of Reconciliation with Indigenous Peoples

In the spirit of reconciliation with Indigenous Peoples in Canada,

I, _____, solemnly pledge to:

1   Commit to honouring the Truth and Reconciliation Commission of Canada's 92nd Call to Action for reconciliation, Business and Reconciliation.

2   Support progressive improvement in our Indigenous relations by encouraging my organization to participate in the Progressive Aboriginal Relations (PAR) program of the Canadian Council for Aboriginal Business.

3   Commit to an in-house community investment strategy that is developed through joint planning with the Indigenous communities involved and aligns with the goals and interests of those communities.

4   Support my organization in ensuring employment opportunities are open to Indigenous candidates and making career development opportunities available.

5   Support my organization in creating a working environment that is inclusive and welcoming for Indigenous employees.

6   Identify contracting or procurement opportunities for Indigenous businesses and economic development corporations.

7   Commit to generating positive and lasting change in my professional and personal life.

Signature _____   Date _____

Terminology:
Guidelines for Usage

||||||||||||||||||||||||||||||||||||||||||||||||||||||||||||||||||||||||||||||||||||||||||||||

L ANGUAGE HAS THE power to respect and honour or hurt and offend. And that is particularly true when you are working across cultures. Within that frame of reference, we respectfully recommend that when working with Indigenous Peoples, you understand how the historical context of certain phrases can affect your communication and relationships.

Here are some clarifying definitions and tips on usage that will come in handy in your communications with and about Indigenous Peoples.

Aboriginal Peoples: This plural noun, used in the *Constitution Act, 1982*, includes First Nations, Métis, and Inuit. So legally, until terminology in the *Constitution Act* is changed, it will always have a place at the terminology table.

Can:

- Use interchangeably with "First Peoples."
- Use interchangeably with "First Nations."
- Use interchangeably with "Indigenous Peoples."

Caution:

- If using interchangeably with "First Nations," note that some First Nations prefer not to be called "Aboriginal Peoples."
- If using this term, always say "Aboriginal Peoples" as opposed to "an Aboriginal" or "Aboriginals" (and *never* "Aborigines," which refers to Indigenous Peoples of Australia).

First Nation(s): A term used to identify Indigenous Peoples of Canada who are neither Métis nor Inuit. The term "First Nation" came into common usage in the 1970s to replace "Indian" and "Indian band," which many found offensive. "First Nations people" includes both status and non-status Indians, so there's a need to be careful with its usage, especially if referring to programs that are specifically for status Indians. (There's more on status and non-status Indians in chapter 7.) There is no legal definition for "First Nation," and it is acceptable as both a noun and a modifier.

Can:

- Use "First Nation" to refer to a single band or the plural "First Nations" for many bands.
- Use "First Nations community" as a respectful alternative phrase.

- Use instead of "Indian" when referring to an individual, for example, "He/she is First Nation."

Caution:

- If using interchangeably with "Aboriginal Peoples," note that some First Nations people don't like the term "Aboriginal Peoples."
- If using interchangeably with "Indigenous Peoples," note that some First Nations may prefer "Indigenous Peoples." For example, First Nations communities in Ontario have expressed publicly and politically that they prefer "Indigenous Peoples."

First Peoples: Another collective term generally used in reference to the population of North America pre-contact and at time of contact.

Indian: The legal identity of an Indigenous person who is registered under the *Indian Act*. One story about the origin of the term "Indian" dates back to Christopher Columbus, who mistakenly thought he had reached the East Indies, so he referred to the people in the lands he visited as *indios*, Spanish for Indian.

Can:

- Use in direct quotations.
- Use when citing titles of books, works of art, etc.
- Use in discussions of history where necessary for clarity and accuracy.
- Use in discussions of some legal/constitutional matters requiring precision in terminology.

- Use in discussions of rights and benefits provided on the basis of Indian status.
- Use in statistical information collected using these categories (e.g., the Census).

Caution:

- The term is otherwise derogatory and outdated and some may take issue with it.

Indigenous Peoples: A plural noun for First Nations, Inuit, and Métis that is growing in popularity in Canada.

Can:

- Use interchangeably with "First Peoples."
- Use interchangeably with "First Nations."
- Use interchangeably with "Aboriginal Peoples."
- Use "Indigenous community" as a respectful alternative phrase.
- Use "an Indigenous People" to refer to a single group, like the Tsleil-Waututh.

Caution:

- If using interchangeably with "First Nations," note that some may prefer "Indigenous Peoples."
- "Indigenous" is never used to refer to an individual—it's an adjective, not a noun, and must be followed by "Peoples," "community," or a similar term. You cannot say "an Indigenous."

Inuit: Refers to Indigenous people in northern Canada, living mainly in Nunavut, Northwest Territories, northern

Quebec, and Labrador. Inuit are not the same as Innu, an Indigenous group that primarily live in northeastern Quebec and southern Labrador. Inuit are not covered by the *Indian Act*. The federal government has entered into several major land claim settlements with Inuit.

Can:

- Use "Inuk" when referring to an individual Inuit person.
- Use "Inuuk" when referring to two people; for three or more people, it is "Inuit."

Caution:

- In the Inuktitut language, "Inuit" translates to "the people" so avoid saying "Inuit People," which would mean "people people." Likewise, since Inuit is a collective noun, it does not need to be preceded by a definite article—don't say "the Inuit live here," just "Inuit live here."
- Never use "Eskimo," as it is considered derogatory.

Métis Peoples: People of mixed Indigenous and European ancestry.

Can:

- Use in reference to those who self-identify as Métis.
- Use "Métis" as a noun and as both plural and singular.
- Use "Métis" as an adjective.

||||||||||||||||||||||||||||||||||||||||||||||||||||||||||||||||||||||||||||||||||||||||||||||||||||||||||||||||

Both "Métis" and "Metis" are in use. Go with the spelling that the people you are working with use. Our main terminology training tip is to "always go with what people call themselves." It requires some research, but it is worth the effort.

||||||||||||||||||||||||||||||||||||||||||||||||||||||||||||||||||||||||||||||||||||||||||||||||||||||||||||||||

Native: An outdated collective term referring to Indians (status and non-status), Métis, and Inuit that has largely been replaced by Indigenous.

||||||||||||||||||||||||||||||||||||||||||||||||||||||||||||||||||||||||||||||||||||||||||||||||||||||||||||||||||||||

Note about Spelling

It's important to always capitalize Indigenous, Aboriginal, First Nations, Inuit, and Métis as a sign of respect, the same way that English, French, Canadian, and Spanish are capitalized.

Glossary

�just visible〔decorative rule〕

Aboriginal consultation: The Crown has a legal duty to engage in meaningful consultation whenever it has reason to believe that its policies or actions, directly or indirectly, might infringe upon actual or claimed Aboriginal Interests, Rights, or Title.

Aboriginal Interests: A broad term referring to the range of rights and entitlements that may arise from long use and occupation of traditional territories by Aboriginal people. Application of common law, statute law, treaty provisions, and the constitutional protection provided to "the existing aboriginal and treaty rights of the aboriginal people of Canada" by Section 35 of the *Constitution Act, 1982*, to the facts of the particular case, determines the scope of "Aboriginal Interests."

Aboriginal Rights:
· Practices, traditions, or customs that are integral to the distinctive culture of an Aboriginal society and were practised prior to European contact, meaning that they were rooted in the pre-contact society

- Must be practised for a substantial period of time to have formed an integral part of the particular Aboriginal society's culture

- Must be an activity that is a central, defining feature that is independently significant to the Aboriginal society

- Must be distinctive, meaning it must be distinguishing and characteristic of that culture

- Must be given priority over all other land uses, after conservation measures

- Must meet a continuity requirement, meaning that the Aboriginal society must demonstrate that the connection with the land in its customs and laws has continued to the present day

- May be the exercise in a modern form of an activity that existed prior to European contact

- May be regulated by government, but only by legislation explicitly directed at a compelling and substantial objective such as the conservation and management of natural resources

- Do not include an activity that solely exists because of the influence of European contact

- Do not include aspects of Aboriginal society that are true of every society such as eating to survive

Aboriginal Title: In general, "Aboriginal Title" refers to the rights of Aboriginal Peoples to the occupation, use, and enjoyment of their land and its resources. The classic legal definition was provided by the Supreme Court of

Canada in *Delgamuukw and Gisday'way*: "aboriginal title encompasses the right to exclusive use and occupation of land; second, aboriginal title encompasses the right to choose to what uses land can be put, subject to the ultimate limit that those uses cannot destroy the ability of the land to sustain future generations of aboriginal peoples; and third, the lands held pursuant to aboriginal title have an inescapable economic component."[1]

Band: The *Indian Act* defines "band," in part, as a body of Indians for whose use and benefit in common lands have been set apart. Each band has its own governing band council, usually consisting of a chief and several councillors. The members of the band usually share common values, traditions, and practices rooted in their language and ancestral heritage. Today, many bands prefer to be known as First Nations. Capitalize "band" when it is part of a specific band, such as Osoyoos Indian Band; otherwise, use lowercase.

Band council: The band's governing body. Community members choose the chief and councillors by election under Section 74 of the *Indian Act*, or through traditional custom. The band council's powers vary with each band.

Colonialism: The exploitation of a people by a larger power.

Elder: Elders are recognized because they have earned the respect of their community through wisdom, harmony, and balance of their actions in their teachings. Elders try to instill respect in their community members for the natural world and teach that the earth is their mother.

Enfranchisement: The process involved in giving up one's status as an Indian; dominant during the era of Indian assimilation practices. In 1985, this practice was terminated by Bill C-31.

Extinguishment: The history of extinguishment of Aboriginal Title has its roots in old or historic treaties that contained the words "cede, release, surrender" of rights, title, and privileges to the lands included within the limits of that particular treaty.

Fiduciary obligation: A legal duty described by the Supreme Court as the obligation of one party to look after the well-being of another. Canada has fiduciary obligations to Aboriginal Peoples, meaning that Canada must consult and negotiate with Aboriginal Peoples whenever their interests are concerned.

Impact and Benefit Agreement (IBA): A broad term used to describe various contractual commitments related to development of land or resources subject to Aboriginal Rights. IBAs usually impose negotiated limits on a project's impacts on the environment, on fish and wildlife, on the land, and on First Nations' traditional use and enjoyment of the same. IBAs usually define a range of negotiated economic and preferential benefits to flow to the First Nation(s) whose lands are to be impacted by the development.

***Indian Act*:** Federal legislation that regulates Indians and reserves and sets out certain federal government powers and responsibilities toward First Nations and their reserved lands. The first *Indian Act* was passed in 1876, although there were a number of pre-Confederation and post-Confederation enactments with respect to Indians and reserves prior to 1876. Since then, it has undergone numerous amendments, revisions, and re-enactments.

Inherent rights: Pre-existing rights that a person is born with into their nation; officially recognized by Canada under Section 35 of the *Constitution Act, 1982*. Aboriginal Peoples of Canada have the right to govern themselves in relation to matters that are internal to their communities; integral to their unique cultures, identities, traditions, languages, and institutions; and with respect to their special relationship to their land and their resources.

Land claims: In 1973, the federal government recognized two broad classes of claims—comprehensive and specific.

- **Comprehensive claims:** A comprehensive claim is a modern treaty made between Indigenous Peoples and the federal, or in some cases provincial, government. They are based on the traditional use and occupancy of land by Indigenous Peoples who did not sign treaties, were not conquered, or did not surrender their lands by any means. Comprehensive claims are based on the assessment that there may be continuing Aboriginal Rights to lands and natural resources. While each claim is unique, frequently these claims include such things as land title; fishing, trapping, and resource rights; and financial compensation—hence "comprehensive."

- **Specific claims:** A specific claim declares grievances over Canada's alleged failures to discharge specific obligations to First Nations groups.

Land claim agreement: A term used by the federal government to refer to a negotiated settlement with a First Nation on lands, land usage, and other rights.

Nation: People united by common descent, history, culture, and language associated with a particular territory.

Oral history: Indigenous Peoples of North America have always relied on oral histories, as opposed to written languages. History is frequently passed through generations in the form of stories, songs, and other oral communications.

Reserve: Defined by the *Indian Act* as a "tract of land, the legal title to which is vested in Her Majesty, that has been set apart by Her Majesty for the use and benefit of a band." A result of the definition of reserve land in the *Indian Act* is that reserve land cannot be privately owned by the band or band members. "Reservation" is an American term.

Self-determination: A major objective of Indigenous Peoples, country-wide, is to gain control over who belongs to their nation. Currently, bands are required to maintain a registry with many of the rules governing membership mandated by the *Indian Act*. As we move into the future, the desire is for communities, rather than a bureaucrat in Ottawa, to decide who their members are. Self-determination is the right to decide who your people are.

Self-government: Long before Europeans arrived in Canada, First Peoples were self-governing. In 1876, when the *Indian Act* went into effect, traditional governance systems were dismantled and alien regulations were imposed in their place. The day-to-day operations of a nation today are directed in accordance with the *Indian Act*. This is a huge problem for nations and their politicians, because it means that while band chief and council are elected by their people, they are accountable to the Department of Crown-Indigenous Relations and Northern Affairs Canada. The preference of many nations would be to change to a system in which the governing leaders are elected and accountable to their people. Such models do exist, and communities with self-government agreements have done well in the nation-building process.

Self-identification: A voluntary, confidential, self-described declaration of Indigenous identity.

Self-reliance: A key objective of Indigenous Peoples. They want the ability to participate in the political and, more importantly, the economic mainstream, without having to rely on federal funding to meet their community needs. In addition to business opportunities, they also want to get into the realm of collecting taxes, royalties, and revenue sharing on land developments, which are viewed as key pieces of the self-reliance puzzle.

Surrender: A formal agreement that confirms the conditions and terms when a First Nation exchanges part of its territory for equitable compensation.

Socio-economic Participation Agreement (SEPA): A synonym for Impact and Benefit Agreement (IBA).

Traditional Ecological Knowledge (TEK): Broadly describes systems for understanding one's environment, based on detailed personal observation and experience and informed by generations of elders. TEK is recognized and used around the world as an important environmental assessment tool.

Traditional territory: The geographic area identified by a First Nation to be the area of land that they and/or their ancestors traditionally occupied or used.

Treaty: An agreement between government and a First Nation that defines the rights of Aboriginal Peoples with respect to lands and resources over a specified area, and it may also define the self-government authority of a First Nation. Modern treaties, once ratified, become part of the law of the land.

Treaty Rights: Rights specified in a treaty. Rights to hunt and fish in traditional territory and to use and occupy reserves are typical Treaty Rights. This concept can have different meanings depending upon the context and perspective of the user. Treaty Rights are constitutionally recognized and affirmed; the terms of treaties take precedence over the other laws and policies in Canada.

Treaty settlement land: The area of land that is part of a treaty and is therefore owned and managed by the First Nation that negotiated the treaty.

Tribal council: Not defined under the *Indian Act*, a tribal council usually represents a group of nations to facilitate the administration and delivery of local services to their members.

Urban reserve: There are two types of urban reserves. One is a reserve that was rural but became urban when a neighbouring town expanded around them; an example is the Musqueam Reserve in Vancouver. The second type of reserve is created when a First Nation acquires a block of land in a city and works through the process of acquiring reserve status for the land.

Usufructuary rights: Communal or community rights to share in the use of property. This concept has been used by the courts in attempting to distinguish between Crown Title and Aboriginal Title.

Additional Resources

||||||||||||||||||||||||||||||||||||||||||||||||||||||||||||||||||||||||||||||||||||||||||||||||||||||

YOU MAY NEED to fill gaps in your own education by learning about Indigenous history, including the critical roles that Indigenous Peoples played in creating Canada and fighting on the side of Canada in two world wars. Taking a reconciliation-focused perspective in your own education can mean addressing some uncomfortable truths, such as the intergenerational impacts of colonization, attempts at assimilation, and cultural genocide—and ensuring that history never repeats itself.

We hope our book has inspired you to continue your learning journey. To that end, we've included some resources to assist you: books, films, and websites. We're not saying these are the only or necessarily the best resources for you, but we have found them of value and we hope you do too.

We haven't included fiction, as there are so many amazing novels and short-story collections by Indigenous writers we wouldn't know where to begin to narrow down the field. One exciting aspect of the boom in Indigenous fiction is that there are now books for all ages.

Indigenous authors, directors, actors, musicians, dancers, artists, and designers alike are enjoying well-deserved exposure and appreciation. There has never been a shortage of talent, but there is now a sense of empowerment in the artistic community, and mainstream Canada is responding and supporting that empowerment.

Books

John Burrows, *Freedom and Indigenous Constitutionalism* (University of Toronto Press, 2016).

Phil Fontaine, Aimée Craft, and the Truth and Reconciliation Commission of Canada, *A Knock on the Door: The Essential History of Residential Schools from the Truth and Reconciliation Commission of Canada* (University of Manitoba Press, 2015).

Daniel Francis, *The Imaginary Indian: The Image of the Indian in Canadian Culture* (Arsenal Pulp Press, 1992).

Gary Geddes, *Medicine Unbundled: A Journey through the Minefields of Indigenous Health Care* (Heritage House, 2017).

Bob Joseph, *21 Things You May Not Know About the Indian Act* (Indigenous Relations Press, 2018).

Daniel Heath Justice, *Why Indigenous Literatures Matter* (Wilfrid Laurier University Press, 2018).

Robin Wall Kimmerer, *Braiding Sweetgrass: Indigenous Wisdom, Scientific Knowledge and the Teachings of Plants* (Milkweed Editions, 2015).

Thomas King, *The Inconvenient Indian: A Curious Account of Native People in North America* (Anchor Canada, 2013).

Thomas King, *The Truth About Stories: A Native Narrative*, CBC Massey Lectures (House of Anansi Press, 2003).

The Kino-nda-niimi Collective, *The Winter We Danced: Voices from the Past, the Future, and the Idle No More Movement* (Arbeiter Ring Publishing, 2014).

John Sutton Lutz, *Makúk: A New History of Aboriginal-White Relations* (UBC Press, 2009).

Arthur Manuel and Grand Chief Ronald Derrickson, *The Reconciliation Manifesto: Recovering the Land, Rebuilding the Economy* (Lorimer, 2017).

Arthur Manuel and Grand Chief Ronald Derrickson, *Unsettling Canada: A National Wake-Up Call* (Between the Lines, 2015).

Lee Maracle, *My Conversations with Canadians* (BookThug, 2017).

Joseph Auguste Merasty, *The Education of Augie Merasty: A Residential School Memoir* (University of Regina Press, 2015).

Edmund Metatawabin with Alexandra Shimo, *Up Ghost River: A Chief's Journey through the Turbulent Waters of Native History* (Vintage Canada, 2015).

Bev Sellars, *They Called Me Number One: Secrets and Survival at an Indian Residential School* (Talonbooks, 2012).

Leanne Betasamosake Simpson, *Dancing on Our Turtle's Back: Stories of Nishnaabeg Re-Creation, Resurgence, and a New Emergence* (Arbeiter Ring Publishing, 2011).

Tanya Talaga, *All Our Relations: Finding the Path Forward*, CBC Massey Lectures (House of Anansi Press, 2018).

Tanya Talaga, *Seven Fallen Feathers: Racism, Death, and Hard Truths in a Northern City* (House of Anansi Press, 2017).

Truth and Reconciliation Commission of Canada, *Final Report of the Truth and Reconciliation Commission of Canada, vol. 1: Summary; Honouring the Truth, Reconciling for the Future* (Lorimer, 2015).

Gregory Younging, *Elements of Indigenous Style: A Guide for Writing By and About Indigenous Peoples* (Brush Education, 2018).

Films

8th Fire (CBC documentary series, 2014).

Bee Nation (Lana Slezic, 2017).

CBQM (Dennis Allen, 2009).

Colonization Road (Michelle St. John, 2017).

Edge of the Knife (Gwaai Edenshaw and
    Helen Haig-Brown, 2018).

First Stories: Two-Spirited (Sharon A. Desjarlais, 2007).

Foster Child (Gil Cardinal, 1987).

Four Sheets to the Wind (Sterlin Harjo, 2007).

Lumaajuuq (Alethea Arnaquq-Baril, 2010).

Nimmikaage (Michelle Latimer, 2015).

The People of the Kattawapiskak River (Alanis Obomsawin, 2012).

Rumble: The Indians Who Rocked the World (Catherine Bain-
    bridge and Alfonso Maiorana, 2017).

Rhymes for Young Ghouls (Jeff Barnaby, 2013).

Smoke Signals (Chris Eyre, 1998).

Websites

Indigenous (CBC News)

Unreserved (CBC Radio)

Reclaimed (CBC Music)

Indigenous Foundations

National Centre for Truth and Reconciliation

Reconciliation Canada

Working Effectively with Indigenous Peoples® (blog)

Notes

||||||||||||||||||||||||

INTRODUCTION

1 Truth and Reconciliation Commission of Canada, *Final Report of the Truth and Reconciliation Commission of Canada, vol. 1: Summary; Honouring the Truth, Reconciling for the Future* (Toronto: Lorimer, 2015).

CHAPTER 1: INDIGENOUS OR ABORIGINAL: DOES IT MATTER?

1 José R. Martínez Cobo, special rapporteur of the Sub-Commission on Prevention of Discrimination and Protection of Minorities, *Study of the Problem of Discrimination against Indigenous Populations, vol. V: Conclusions, Proposals and Recommendations* (New York: United Nations, 1987), 29, https://documents-dds-ny.un.org/doc/UNDOC/GEN/N87/121/00/PDF/N8712100.pdf.

CHAPTER 2: CULTURAL DIVERSITY AMONG INDIGENOUS PEOPLES

1 Thomas King, *The Inconvenient Indian: A Curious Account of Native People in North America* (Toronto: Anchor Canada, 2013), prologue.

2 As defined by the *British North America Act, 1867*; the *Indian Act, 1876*; and the *Constitution Act, 1982*, respectively.

3 Statistics Canada, "Aboriginal Population Profile, 2016 Census," www12.statcan.gc.ca/census-recensement/2016/dp-pd/abpopprof/index.cfm.

4 "Reserve" is the Canadian term; "reservation" is the American term.

5 Statistics Canada, "Aboriginal Population Profile, 2016 Census."

6 Canada, Royal Commission on Aboriginal Peoples, *Report, vol. 4: Perspectives and Realities* (Ottawa: Minister of Supply and Services Canada, 1996), 538.

CHAPTER 3: INDIGENOUS IDENTITY AND GOVERNANCE STRUCTURE

1 As far as we can determine, around 200 First Nations in Canada hold elections under Section 74 of the *Indian Act.*
2 "Justice Minister Wilson-Raybould Tells AFN to Prepare for Future beyond the *Indian Act*," APTN National News, July 25, 2017, https://aptnnews.ca/2017/07/25/justice-minister-wilson-raybould-tells-afn-to-prepare-for-future-beyond-the-indian-act.
3 Amy Smart, Canadian Press, "*Indian Act* to Blame for Pipeline Gridlock in Northern B.C.: Federal Minister," *The Province,* Jan. 25, 2019, https://theprovince.com/pmn/news-pmn/canada-news-pmn/indian-act-to-blame-for-pipeline-gridlock-in-northern-b-c-federal-minister.

CHAPTER 4: CIRCLE OF UNDERSTANDING: RECOGNIZING INDIGENOUS WORLDVIEWS

1 John Ralston Saul, *The Comeback* (Toronto: Penguin, 2015), 226.
2 Canada, Royal Commission on Aboriginal Peoples, *Report, vol. 2: Restructuring the Relationship* (Ottawa: Minister of Supply and Services Canada, 1996), 427.

CHAPTER 5: WORKING WITH COMMUNITIES: EMPLOYMENT BARRIERS AND OTHER ISSUES

1 Public Archives of Canada, Scott Papers, RG 10 vol. 6810, file 473, vol. 12, *Hearings Testimony, 1921–22.*
2 *An Act to Amend and Consolidate the Laws Respecting Indians (Indian Act),* 1876, Terms 3.12, aadnc-aandc.gc.ca/eng/1100100010252/1100100010254.
3 Duncan McCue, "News Stereotypes of Aboriginal Peoples," *Reporting in Indigenous Communities*, http://riic.ca/the-guide/at-the-desk/news-stereotypes-of-aboriginal-peoples.
4 J. Reading, *The Crisis of Chronic Disease among Aboriginal Peoples: A Challenge for Public Health, Population Health and Social Policy* (Victoria: University of Victoria Centre for Aboriginal Health Research, 2009).
5 Statistics Canada, "Aboriginal Population Profile, 2016 Census."
6 Statistics Canada, "First Nations People, Métis and Inuit in Canada: Diverse and Growing Populations," March 20, 2018, www150.statcan.gc.ca/n1/pub/89-659-x/89-659-x2018001-eng.htm.

7   Sheila Block, "Canada's Population Is Changing but Income Inequality Remains a Problem," *Behind the Numbers,* October 27, 2017, http://behindthenumbers.ca/2017/10/27/population-changing-income-inequality-remains.

8   Julie Renato, "Adult Correctional Statistics in Canada, 2015/2016," Statistics Canada, www.150.statcan.gc.ca/n1/pub/85-002-x/2017001/article/14700-eng.htm.

9   Assembly of First Nations Environmental Stewardship Unit, "A Statistical Profile on the Health of First Nations in Canada for the Year 2000," discussion paper, March 2008, 7, www.afn.ca/uploads/files/rp-discussion_paper_re_childrens_health_and_the_environment.pdf.

10 Statistics Canada, "First Nations People, Métis and Inuit in Canada: Diverse and Growing Populations."

11 Dominion of Canada, *Annual Report of the Department of Indian Affairs for the Year Ended March 31, 1936* (Ottawa: J.O. Patenaude, I.S.O., Printer to the King's Most Excellent Majesty, 1937), 10.

12 "Among non-Aboriginal manufacturing workers in the core-age group, employment declined by 8% or 14,000 jobs, with the bulk of the jobs lost in Ontario. At the same time, manufacturing employment among their Aboriginal counterparts fell by 30% or 7,000 jobs, with jobs mostly lost in the Western provinces. In the construction industry, Aboriginal employment fell by 16% or 4,000 jobs, while it decreased by 5% or 45,000 jobs among non-Aboriginal workers." Statistics Canada, *2012 Canada Year Book* (11-402-X), "Aboriginal Peoples," www150.statcan.gc.ca/n1/pub/11-402-x/2011000/chap/ap-pa/ap-pa-eng.htm.

13 John Richards, "Census 2016: Where Is the Discussion about Indigenous Education?," *Globe and Mail,* Dec. 13, 2017, www.theglobeandmail.com/opinion/census-2016-where-is-the-discussion-about-indigenous-education/article37313434.

14 Statistics Canada, "Census in Brief: The Housing Conditions of Aboriginal People in Canada," Oct. 25, 2017, www12.statcan.gc.ca/census-recensement/2016/as-sa/98-200-x/2016021/98-200-x2016021-eng.cfm.

15 Fiscal Realities Economists, "Reconciliation: Growing Canada's Economy by $27.7 Billion; Background and Methods Paper," prepared for the National Aboriginal Economic Development Board, Nov. 2016, 17, http://naedb-cndea.com/reports/naedb_report_reconciliation_27_7_billion.pdf.

CHAPTER 6: NATION TO NATION:
UNDERSTANDING TREATIES, THEN AND NOW

1   Bob Rae, "The Gap Between Historic Treaty Peoples and Everyone
     Else," Remarks for the University of Regina, Oct. 30, 2014, 6.
2   Royal Commission on Aboriginal Peoples, *Report, vol. 5: Renewal: A
     Twenty-Year Commitment* (Ottawa: Minister of Supply and Services
     Canada, 1996), 1.
3   Royal Commission on Aboriginal Peoples, *Report, vol. 5: Renewal: A
     Twenty-Year Commitment*, 1.
4   *Calder et al. v. Attorney-General of British Columbia*, [1973] S.C.R. 313.
5   Royal Commission on Aboriginal Peoples, *Report, vol. 5: Renewal: A
     Twenty-Year Commitment*, 1.
6   Canada, *Aboriginal Self-Government: The Government of Canada's
     Approach to Implementation of the Inherent Right and the Negotiation of
     Aboriginal Self-Government* (Ottawa: Minister of Public Works and
     Government Services Canada, 1995), 3.
7   *Sechelt Indian Band Self-Government Act* (S.C. 1986, c. 27).
8   This agreement led to the *Nunavut Act* (S.C. 1993, c. 28) and *Nunavut
     Land Claims Agreement Act* (S.C. 1993, c. 29).
9   *Nisga'a Final Agreement Act* (S.C. 2000, c. 7).
10   *An Act to Give Effect to the Westbank First Nation Self Government
     Agreement* (S.C. 2004, c. 17).
11   Nisga'a Lisims Government, "Understanding the Treaty,"
     www.nisgaanation.ca/understanding-treaty.
12   Royal Commission on Aboriginal Peoples, *Report, vol. 5: Renewal:
     A Twenty-Year Commitment*, 56.

CHAPTER 7: ISN'T IT TRUE THAT...? MYTH VS. REALITY

1   The full text of the *United Nations Declaration on the Rights of
     Indigenous Peoples* can be found at www.un.org/development/
     desa/indigenouspeoples/declaration-on-the-rights-of-indigenous-
     peoples.html.
2   Statistics Canada, "Aboriginal Population Profile, 2016 Census."
3   Brian Slattery, "A Taxonomy of Aboriginal Rights," in *Let Right Be
     Done: Aboriginal Title, the Calder Case, and the Future of Indigenous
     Rights*, ed. Hamar Foster, Heather Raven, and Jeremy Webber
     (Vancouver: UBC Press, 2007), 111–28.
4   United Nations Office of the High Commissioner on Human
     Rights, *Convention on the Prevention and Punishment of the Crime
     of Genocide*, entry into force: Jan. 12, 1951, www.ohchr.org/en/
     professionalinterest/pages/crimeofgenocide.aspx.

5 CBC News, "Senator Murray Sinclair Responds to Lynn Beyak's Defence of Residential Schools," March 29, 2017, www.cbc.ca/news/politics/murray-sinclair-lynn-beyak-residential-schools-1.4045465.

CHAPTER 8: RESPECT: A PATH TOWARD WORKING EFFECTIVELY WITH INDIGENOUS PEOPLES®

1 In court records, *Delgamuukw v. British Columbia.* This expanded version of the case title acknowledges the contributions of both the Gitxsan and Wet'suwet'en Nations to the case.
2 *Tsleil-Waututh Nation v. Canada (Attorney General),* 2018 FCA 153.
3 If you are working with a community on Vancouver Island, be sure to do your research, as the Douglas Treaties cover some territories.
4 Gregory Younging, *Elements of Indigenous Style: A Guide for Writing By and About Indigenous Peoples* (Brush Education, 2018), 91.
5 Ronald Wright, *Stolen Continents: The "New World" Through Indian Eyes* (Toronto; Penguin Books, 1993), 4.
6 Chief Justice Lamer in *R. v. Van der Peet,* [1996] 2 SCR 507, para 30.
7 Canada, *House of Commons Debates*, 5th Parliament, 1st Session, (May 9, 1883), 1107–1108.

CHAPTER 9: THE PERSONAL SIDE OF RECONCILIATION

1 United Nations Office of the High Commissioner on Human Rights, "End of Mission Statement by Dubravka Šimonović, United Nations Special Rapporteur on Violence against Women, Its Causes and Consequences—Official Visit to Canada," April 23, 2018, www.ohchr.org/en/NewsEvents/Pages/DisplayNews.aspx?NewsID=22981.
2 Orange Shirt Day: Every Child Matters, "Phyllis' Story: The Original Orange Shirt," www.orangeshirtday.org/phyllis-story.html.

CONCLUSION

1 Truth and Reconciliation Commission of Canada, *Final Report of the Truth and Reconciliation Commission of Canada, vol. I: Summary: Honouring the Truth, Reconciling for the Future* (Toronto: Lorimer, 2015), 6.
2 Chief Dr. Robert Joseph, "Healing a Nation Through Truth and Reconciliation," TEDxEastVan, May 24, 2016, https://youtu.be/rJQgpuLqILI.

APPENDIX III: GLOSSARY

1 *Delgamuukw v. British Columbia,* [1997] 3 SCR 1010, para 166.

Index

‖‖‖‖‖‖‖‖‖‖‖‖‖‖‖‖‖‖

About the Authors

〰〰〰〰〰〰〰〰〰〰〰〰〰〰〰〰〰〰〰〰〰〰〰〰〰〰〰〰〰〰

Bob Joseph

Bob Joseph, founder and president of Indigenous Corporate Training Inc., has provided training on Indigenous relations since 1994. As a certified Master Trainer, Bob has assisted both individuals and organizations in building Indigenous relations. His Canadian clients include all levels of government, Fortune 500 companies, financial institutions, including the World Bank, small and medium corporate enterprises, and Indigenous Peoples. He has worked internationally for clients in the United States, Guatemala, Peru, and New Caledonia in the South Pacific. In 2006, Bob co-facilitated a worldwide Indigenous Peoples' round table in Switzerland, which included participants from the United Nations; Australia; New Zealand; North, Central, and South America; Africa; and the Philippines.

Bob has worked as an associate professor at Royal Roads University and is routinely a guest lecturer at other academic institutions. He has an educational background in business administration and international trade and in

May 2001 was profiled in an annual feature called "Training: The New Guard 2001" by the American Society of Training and Development. Bob was one of nine trainers selected for the feature from over 70,000 members who come from more than 100 countries and 15,000 organizations.

Bob is the developer of a multi-layer suite of training courses:

- Working Effectively with Indigenous Peoples®
- Indigenous Awareness
- Indigenous Relations
- Indigenous Consultation & Engagement
- Creating an Indigenous Engagement Plan (co-authored)
- How to Negotiate with Indigenous Peoples
- Working with UNDRIP

Bob is the author or co-author of books and resources relating to working with Indigenous Peoples, including:

- *21 Things You May Not Know About the Indian Act*
- *Indigenous Relations: Insights, Tips, and Suggestions to Make Reconciliation a Reality*
- *Working Effectively with Indigenous Peoples®,* 4th edition
- *Aboriginal Community Engagement: Handbook for the British Columbia & Yukon Chamber of Mines* (co-authored)

Bob is an Indigenous person, or more specifically a status Indian. He is an initiated member of the Hamatsa Society, has inherited a chief's seat in the Gayaxala (thunderbird) clan, first clan of the Gwawa'enuxw, and will host his inaugural potlatch as chief in 2019. Bob's chief name is K'axwsumala'galis, which loosely translated means "whale who emerges itself from the water and presents itself to the world."

Cynthia F. Joseph

Cindy Joseph is an integral part of the Indigenous Corporate Training Inc. team. She is a co-author of our books and the main developer of the online training programs. Cindy received her Bachelor of Laws degree from the University of British Columbia in 1990 and was called to the bar in 1991. She maintained a general law practice consecutively on the North Shore of Vancouver, Bowen Island, and Burnaby. While practising law, Cindy began using her experiences as a faculty member at Capilano University in the highly recognized Paralegal Program. The combination of her legal degree and her experience providing instruction in class and in an online format has been invaluable in developing the online training programs that we offer. Cindy's research skills and educational background ensure that our Working Effectively with Indigenous Peoples® books and training manuals are up-to-date and reliable.

About Indigenous Corporate Training Inc.

⁞⁞⁞

Bob talks fast and provides an insight in every breath. Make sure you come with an empty mind because it will be full when you're done.

C.H.

INDIGENOUS CORPORATE TRAINING Inc. (ICT) is a global training company committed to working collaboratively with regional, national, and international clients to provide a broad range of performance improvement training services geared specifically at helping individuals and organizations work effectively with Indigenous Peoples. We at ICT recognize that organizations and their shareholders are interested in demonstrated results of how performance improvement consulting expenditures contribute to the effectiveness of an organization. We go to great lengths to ensure there is a demonstrated link between performance improvement consulting measures and increased organizational effectiveness. ICT knows that funds spent on performance improvement training are at the expense of other initiatives, and we understand that the performance improvement must be the main driver of the work we do.

ICT provides public, private, and online training. Our training options are posted on www.ictinc.ca. To arrange for private training, please contact our office at info@ictinc.ca. If you would like additional information and opportunities to learn and share ideas with others, subscribe to *Indigenous Relations Bulletin*, our free, monthly newsletter available at www.ictinc.ca/newsletter-sign-up.

NATIONAL BESTSELLER

"This straightforward book is an invaluable resource. There is much for non-Indigenous people to learn and to do. But equally important, there is much to unlearn and to undo. The time is right for this book." Shelagh Rogers, O.C., *Truth and Reconciliation Commission of Canada Honorary Witness*

"This pocket-size primer is a perfect introduction to a troubling legacy with which Canadians continue to wrestle." *Publishers Weekly* (starred review)

THE ESSENTIAL GUIDE to understanding the *Indian Act* and its repercussions on generations of Indigenous Peoples.

A key way to improve your Indigenous relations is by educating yourself on the *Indian Act*, which has dictated and constrained the lives of Indigenous Peoples since its creation in 1876. *21 Things You May Not Know About the Indian Act* examines how Indigenous Peoples can return to self-government, self-determination, and self-reliance—and why doing so would result in a better country for every Canadian.